Longman Scienceworld

Teachers Book A

GENERAL EDITOR: BRENDA PRESTT

SCIENCE THROUGH INFANT TOPICS

ENID HARGRAVE AND JANET BROOKS

sour

sweet

Longman

General Editor:
Dr Brenda Prestt M.B.E.
who was a member of the APU Science Steering Group and editor of A
Language in Science. She is a contributor to the Open University Prima
Science course, and was Director of the Centre for Industry, Science,
Technology Education Liaison based at Manchester Polytechnic.

Authors of the infant material in *Longman Scienceworld:*
Enid Hargrave
who was formerly Head Teacher
and
Janet Brooks
who is Deputy Head
of Chuckery Infants School, Walsall, West Midlands.

Illustrators: Ann Baum, David Brown, John Fraser, David McKee, Mark
Peppé and Chris Williamson.
Cover photograph: Chris Wright.

LONGMAN GROUP LIMITED
Longman House, Burnt Mill, Harlow, Essex CM20 2JE, England
and Associated Companies throughout the world

First published 1986
Fourth impression 1989
ISBN 0 582 18610 2
Typeset in 'Monophoto' Univers 689
Produced by Longman Group (FE) Ltd
Printed in Hong Kong

CONTENTS

LONGMAN SCIENCEWORLD

This science scheme covers the Primary years – from when a child enters school up to the age of eleven. The books for the scheme are:

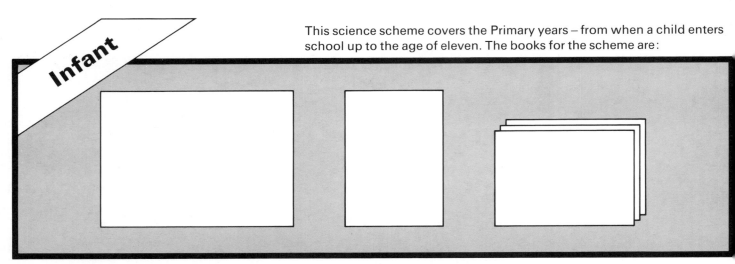

Year 1 *Starter Book A* accompanied by *Science through Infant Topics Teachers' Book A* and *Record Sheets*

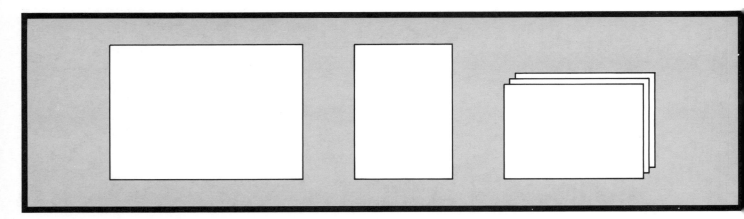

Year 2 *Starter Book B* accompanied by *Science through Infant Topics Teachers' Book B* and *Record Sheets*

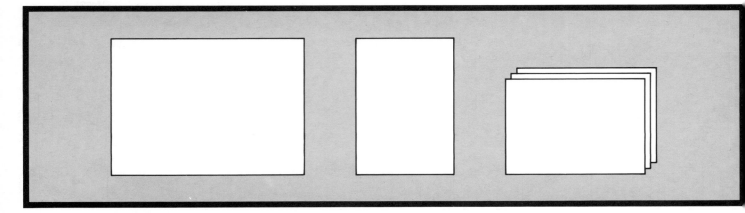

Year 3 *Starter Readers* (set of four) accompanied by *Science through Infant Topics Teachers' Book C* and *Record Sheets*

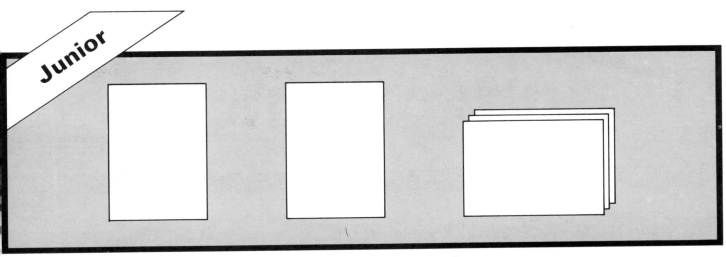

Year 1 *Junior Pupils' Book 1* accompanied by *Junior Teachers' Book 1 and 2* and *Record Sheets*

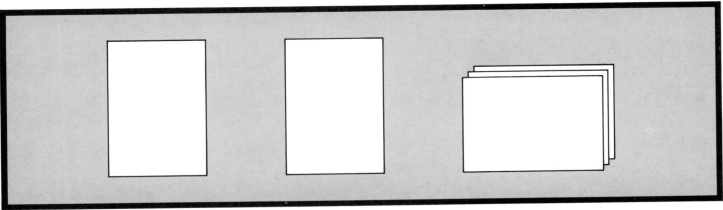

Year 2 *Junior Pupils' Book 2* accompanied by *Junior Teachers' Book 1 and 2* and *Record Sheets*

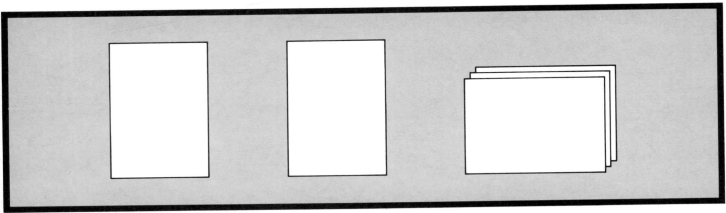

Year 3 *Junior Pupils' Book 3* accompanied by *Junior Teachers' Book 3 and 4* and *Record Sheets*

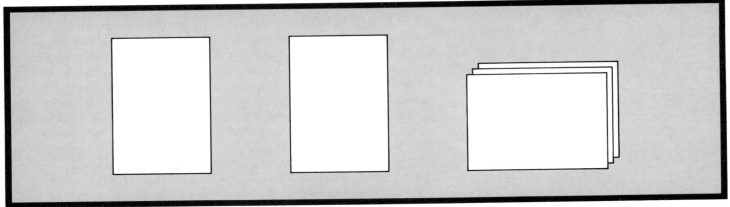

Year 4 *Junior Pupils' Book 4* accompanied by *Junior Teachers' Book 3 and 4* and *Record Sheets*

INTRODUCTION

This science scheme is firmly rooted in the infant curriculum of most schools. The topics have been carefully selected in response to children's interests, with the purpose of arousing their curiosity and fostering their enthusiasm.

Teachers use topic work to provide a wide range of learning experiences for children. The science which has always been there but has, too often, been unrecognised or neglected is presented here.

As the science in the scheme arises from familiar topics, you will be able to use the science activities in your curriculum without having to make uncomfortable changes or adjustments. Science must arise from the normal work of the infant classroom and be fully integrated with it if it is to become an accepted part of the infant curriculum and if it is to succeed. The link between science and mathematics is particularly close, so where appropriate, mathematical activities have been included. At each level, these have been carefully matched with the work normally covered in the infant classroom, where one of the more popular mathematics schemes such as *Nuffield Maths 5–11* is being used.

As you use the science activities with your children, you will find a wealth of opportunities for language work. Language is an important means by which understanding is explored and developed, and

Learning through water play

Helping the plumber

experiences shared and communicated. The development of science skills is inseparable from the development of language skills.

Not only should children experience science as an exciting way of investigating the world, but they should also grow up realising that science is always around us. With *Longman Scienceworld*, the children come to know the characters in a fictional street, Newton Street, which is used throughout the scheme. The different people in Newton Street use science in their everyday affairs and in their jobs.

Children are great inventors and take delight in making and doing. Their simple making and doing activities provide roots for the later development of technological ability. Making and doing continually raises questions about which materials to use and what they will do, how to make stronger structures and how to make things move – all questions which require scientific investigations to provide the answers. For young children, there is a lot to be gained by developing making and doing activities alongside science activities.

One of the joys of teaching young children is observing their progress and development. Children progress at very different rates and responding to the individual's needs makes great demands on the teacher. Perhaps even more difficult is the devising of appropriate activities which will help children to progress.

The activities over the three infant years are arranged so that there is a steady structured progression. In each year, the work is pitched at two levels, each corresponding to half a year. Within a level, the activities are of approximately equal difficulty, so that the topics can be used in an order different from that in which they are presented. It should be noted, however, that at each level it is assumed that the children have achieved the objectives of the previous level(s).

The topics introduced in the infant years are described below.

	Homes	People who help us	Special times	Shopping	Genera
Year 1 Level 1			Harvest Bonfire night Christmas Winter	Clothes	What can I do?
Year 1 Level 2	The bathroom	The cook The caretaker	Spring School holidays		
Year 2 Level 1	Jobs in the kitchen	The post		The shoe shop The supermarket The sweet shop	Pets
Year 2 Level 2		The police The firefighter Milk	Easter		The park
Year 3 Level 1	In the garden Jobs in the house		Hallowe'en Celebrations	The newsagent	Sports and games
Year 3 Level 2				Fabrics	Transport Animals The farm Weather

Deciding whether children are ready to move from one level to another is not easy but we hope that the *Record Sheets* will help you to focus on specific aspects of the children's achievements and assist you in deciding where individual children need help.

As a final word, science for young children is about doing and finding out. Science for you is about providing the opportunities and sharing the children's enjoyment and enthusiasm.

The next pages describe the general structure of the books for *Science through Infant Topics*. Logically, you should carry on and read them but, if you have *Starter Book A* and you want to dive straight in, you could turn to Using the books, on page xii.

The rationale for our approach to science in the infant school is discussed more fully in the Extensions.

THE STRUCTURE OF THE BOOKS

Starter Books and Readers

The *Starter Books* for years 1 and 2 are teachers' books. They contain large pictures, each of which introduces a topic. Each picture is accompanied by a set of teachers' prompts which enables the teacher to introduce, in the context of the topic, science activities and short discussions about people and their jobs and occupations. In year 3, pupils' illustrated reading books replace the *Starter Books*. The four *Starter Readers* provide starting points for discussion and activities, in the same way that the pictures in the *Starter Books* did previously.

The *Starter Books* and *Readers* set the scene for science learning.

Teachers' Books

The *Teachers' Books* contain all the information needed by the teacher to:
    carry out the Science activities,
    introduce Making and doing activities,
    and extend the topics with Further activities.
In addition, the *Teachers' Books* contain a discussion of the rationale for the scheme and other reference material.

Levels

The work for each year is set at two levels. The work of level 1 approximates to the first half of the year and level 2 the second half of the year.

Topics

In year 1, at level 1, the topics are:	key letter	At level 2, the topics are:	
Harvest	H	Spring	S
Bonfire night	Bo	The bathroom	B
What can I do?	Wh	The cook	Co
Christmas	C	The caretaker	Ca
Clothes	Cl	School holidays	Sc
Winter	W		

Topic guides

At the beginning of each topic in the *Teachers' Books*, you will find a diagram which sets out the main objectives of the Science activities based on that topic, and gives page references for these and for the Making and doing activities. Reference is also provided for the suggestions for Further activities. For discussion about People and their jobs and occupations, reference is made to the *Starter Book*.

Topic activities described in Teachers' Books A and B

Science activities

Title
Each Science activity has a short title, the main purpose of which is to aid staff room communication. The activity numbers in conjunction with the topic key letters provide a means of identifying specific activities.

Main objective
The main objective for each activity is clearly stated. It is these objectives which form the backbone of the scheme.

Materials required
These are listed as fully as possible; it is difficult to be precise about quantities since these will depend on the size of your group.

Description of the activity
The description provides a detailed guide to the presentation of the activity in the classroom and indicates points which should be emphasised. The implication throughout is that doing is only part of the activity; the talking throws light on the doing.

At some points where you might need further clarification about methods (e.g. bean sprout growing) or presentation, there are references to the Extensions.

Very occasionally, it is suggested that children should taste items of food. Wherever this occurs, a warning is given in the text and you should make sure that the children understand that they should only taste what they know is food, and only if you, the teacher, give permission.

Making and doing activities

In each case, children are given a problem which has many possible solutions. All the problems require the children to make something. The presentation of the problem to the children is described step by step.
1 The problem
2 Exploring the problem
3 Ideas for solving the problem
4 Making
5 Evaluating

The sequence for problem solving is rarely as neat and tidy as this in practice, but it helps to establish a good approach to problem solving activity, which can be built on and developed. The suggested structure should be used as a guide rather than as a prescription. (The rationale for this approach to making and doing will be found in the Extensions.)

At a practical level, the materials required are specified as far as possible but quantities will depend on the size of your group.

Further activities

The topic guide which introduces each topic indicates that the science and other activities are part of a more extended scheme based on the topic. The section entitled Further activities is intended to give you some useful ideas which you might like to incorporate in your work in other areas of the curriculum. They are just ideas but it is hoped you will find them helpful.

Topic activities described in the Starter Books

People and their jobs and occupations

In these sections, the *Starter Book* pictures are used to bring out various aspects of what people do with their time. This is in itself of importance and interest but, in the context of the scheme, it is intended also to show how much people use and need science in everyday life.

Each of these sections has two parts. The first is a series of discussion points arising from the picture. By a series of numbers, reference is made to the second part, which consists of ideas to be developed.

Increasingly, there are links between the Science activities and what people need to be able to do or to understand in their lives. This is brought out not only in discussions about People and their jobs and occupations but also at appropriate points in the Science activities.

USING THE BOOKS

Preparation

Step 1
Refer to *Teachers' Book A* and select the topic you wish to use, e.g. Harvest.

Step 2
Locate the topic in
a) *Teachers' Book A*   page 3
b) *Starter Book A*   page 8

Step 3
Refer to the *Teachers' Book* for instructions and requirements for each of the Science activities.

Step 4
Decide which Science activities you wish to do and collect the necessary materials.

Step 5
In *Starter Book A* look at the picture and read the teacher prompts.

With your class

Step 1

Show the children the picture in *Starter Book A* and use the Discussion points to introduce the discussion about People and their jobs and occupations. Extension G on page 132 offers guidance for this discussion.

Step 2

Use the Starting point which will lead you into the first of the Science activities which you have selected.

Step 3

Refer to the *Teachers' Book* for instructions for carrying out the activity with the children.
You can work through as many of the activities as you wish in a similar way.

Step 4

Refer to the *Teachers' Book* for instructions for the Making and doing activity associated with the topic.

Step 5

Refer to the *Teachers' Book* for suggestions for Further activities.

Recording progress

Ongoing accurate records are an essential part of ensuring that children's experience of science is progressive and developmental; to assist teachers in keeping records, sets of pupils' *Record Sheets* are available. There is a record sheet for each level so that a complete record of progress can be maintained for each pupil and accompany him or her from one class to the next. Extension H on page 134 gives fuller information about the *Record Sheets*.

LEVEL 1: TOPICS

Harvest

Bonfire night

What can I do?

Christmas

Clothes

Winter

INTRODUCTION TO LEVEL 1

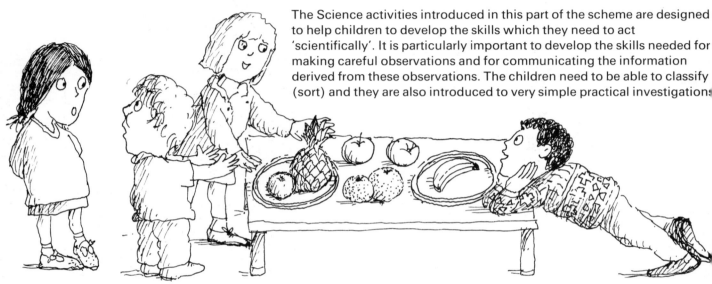

The Science activities introduced in this part of the scheme are designed to help children to develop the skills which they need to act 'scientifically'. It is particularly important to develop the skills needed for making careful observations and for communicating the information derived from these observations. The children need to be able to classify (sort) and they are also introduced to very simple practical investigations.

The content of some of the activities involving observation and classification may not appear to be 'scientific' in the conventional sense; however, our purpose at this stage is not to teach the children science content. It is rather to present them with the opportunities to develop those science skills which will later provide them with the means to explore and understand science content for themselves. Without this active involvement, children acquire a picture of science which is not only sterile but also false.

At level 1, the children describe their observations orally. The development of appropriate vocabulary and opportunities to use that vocabulary are of the utmost importance in the development of science skills and understanding.

Some of the activities link up with work you are likely to be doing in mathematics. You should find that this not only helps the children in their scientific development but that it also enhances their understanding of mathematics.

Talking and doing

2

 Language

Mathematics

Physical education

Creative arts

Science

Science activities

Introduction

Science activities

The Science activities associated with this topic are very simple ones which are designed to help children develop particularly their abilities to observe and investigate colour, shape, texture and taste. At the same time, the children are encouraged to talk about their observations and discoveries, and develop their vocabulary. They are also given opportunities to develop ideas about sorting and making sets, and to carry out simple ordering tasks.

Investigations are suggested to explore 'What happens when . . .?'. These are not experiments in the formal sense but they introduce children to finding out in a practical way.

Making and doing activities

The problem for the child is:

'Can you make a bag to carry fruit home from the fruit shop?'
This problem poses questions in a very simple fashion about purpose, materials and methods of construction. It introduces a way of working which is developed throughout the scheme. This technological approach is discussed in more detail in Extension F on page 129. You will find it useful to read this section before embarking on the Making and doing activities.

Harvest   Science activities

Activity H1—Fruit colour

Observing the colour and shape of fruits

You need:
a selection of fruit of various colours, with more than one of some colours, e.g. banana and lemon.

You might like to set up a fruit table. The fruit will be needed for subsequent Harvest activities. You could include a variety of fruit: two or three each of green apples, red apples, bananas, lemons, oranges and pears; a few green grapes; a few purple grapes; a peach; a yellow melon; a pineapple.

1 Let the children handle a selection of fruit and make comments about it.
2 Pick out a banana and ask the children to tell you about its shape and colour.
3 Ask the children to pick out all the yellow fruits and put them by the banana.
4 Move the other fruit to one side for the moment and let the children handle the yellow fruit.
5 Ask the children how the fruits are different. Encourage them to mention shape, size, smell and texture.
6 Ask the children how the fruits are the same. From their comments, pick out and emphasise colour.
7 Now return to the other fruits and help the children to sort them for colour. Let the children practise naming the fruits and colours as long as their interest lasts.

Activity H2—Fruit texture

Observing the texture of fruits

You need:

green apples; red apples; bananas; oranges; a peach; a pineapple; two sorting circles.

1 Let the children pass the fruit round and notice how it feels. Encourage them to comment.
2 Ask the children to put the fruit that feels rough in one sorting circle and the fruit that feels smooth in the other circle.
3 Count the members of each set with the children and ask which set has more and which has less.
4 You could do the same for hairy/not hairy, sticky/not sticky or any other texture quality which the children notice. Always encourage discussion about which fruits belong in which set and why.
5 Play a game to see which children can identify each fruit by holding it behind their backs and stroking its skin.

Activity H3—Fruit shape

Observing and investigating the shape of fruits

You need:

two bananas; two lemons; two oranges; two pears; a knife; four plates; a smooth board which can be propped up to make a slope to roll the fruit down.

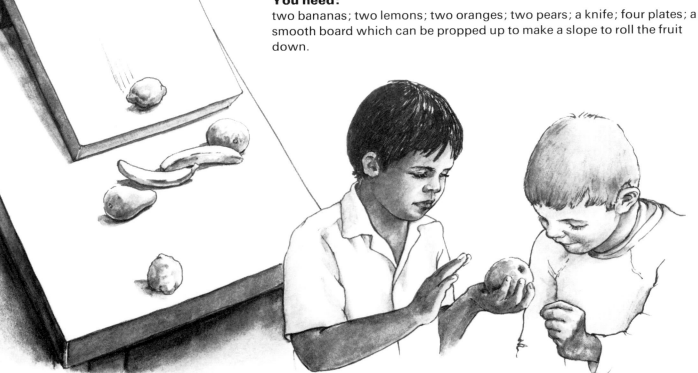

1 Let the children hold the fruit and ask them about the shapes. They may use words like 'long', 'thin', 'fat', 'wide', 'narrow', 'curved', 'ends', 'corners'.
2 Let the children find out what happens when fruits are put at the top of a slope. Make a slope by propping up the smooth board and let the children try each fruit in turn. Ask the children if it matters which way round the fruits are placed. Let them investigate and find out for themselves. Much discussion can be centred on the pear and why it rolls in the way that it does.
3 Take the two pears. Cut one pear from end to end and the other across the middle. When the children have had time to examine them, get them to compare the cross-sectional shapes.
4 Do the same with the oranges, lemons and bananas.
5 Ask the children to remember which fruit rolled down the slope whichever way round it was placed. Then ask them what was special about the shapes when the oranges were cut in different directions.

Activity H4—Fruit smell

Observing the smell of fruits

You need:

a banana; a lemon; an apple; a knife; three plates.

1 Let the children smell the lemon, apple and banana.
2 Now peel the fruits and put the peel on one side. Let the children smell the peeled fruits and ask if the smell is different in any way. Perhaps it is stronger or weaker.
3 Put the fruits on one side and let the children smell the peel. Again ask if the smell is different in any way.
4 When the children have finished, ask them to smell their fingers and tell you which fruit they can smell.

Activity H5—Fruit taste

Observing the taste of fruits

You need:

sour apples; sweet apples; lemons; oranges – enough for the children to taste; a knife; four plates.

Sweet and sour

Warning

This activity involves tasting.
You must emphasise to the children that we only taste things which we know are food. We never taste anything else. They must not taste anything in the classroom unless you tell them to do so. Make sure that the activity is carried out under hygienic conditions – wash hands, use a table cloth, etc.

1 Let the children watch you cut some apples – some downwards and some across. Show the children the pips and save them for Activity H7. Cut up the apples into smaller pieces, and put the sour apples on one plate and the sweet apples on another.
2 Ask the children whether they like apples and whether they think apples taste sweet or sour. Let them take a piece of apple from the 'sour plate' to taste. Ask them whether it is sweet or sour.
3 Do the same with the sweet apples.
4 Now repeat this with an orange on one plate and a lemon on the other. Point out to the children that you do not need to cut oranges and lemons into segments – they come pre-packed! Ask them where the pips are and save them.
5 When you have finished, ask the children whether apples are sweet or sour and then whether oranges are sweet or sour.

Activity H6—Brown apples

Investigating what happens when cut apple is exposed to the air

You need:
two or three kinds of sweet apples, both red and green; green sour apples – enough for the children to taste; a knife; a plate for each kind of apple; a blindfold.

Warning

This activity involves tasting.
You must emphasise to the children that we only taste things which we know are food. We never taste anything else. They must not taste anything in the classroom unless you tell them to do so. Make sure that the activity is carried out under hygienic conditions – wash hands, use a table cloth, etc.

1 Take two or three kinds of apples – red and green sweet apples and green sour apples. Cut them up and place pieces of them on separate plates. Label the plates if necessary. Let the children look at them and encourage them to notice the whiteness of the fruit.
2 Leave the fruit exposed to the air and let the children observe what happens. (Different kinds of apples may brown at different rates. When apples are exposed to the air, certain substances (chemicals) which they contain react with the oxygen in the air and this results in a colour change: white becomes brown. The rate and extent of the browning depends on how much of these substances is present in the particular variety of apple. Browning can be prevented, for example, by sprinkling the apple with lemon juice. This is for your information and might help you answer any questions.)
3 Ask the children if they think that the apple will taste different when it is brown. Let them taste pieces of freshly cut apple and pieces of brown apple. Does it taste different? Could they tell which apple was brown by its taste?
4 If they say, 'Yes', blindfold one of the children and see if he or she can distinguish between brown apple and fresh apple just by taste – and, of course, between sweet apple and sour apple.

7

Activity H7—Pips and stones

Observing and sorting by texture and size – fruit pips and stones

You need:
pips and stones from fruits; a sorting tray.

1 Let the children sort the pips into a sorting tray. Put one of each kind into the separate compartments first, so that the children can match them.

2 Ask the children to choose one of each type and place them on the table. Help the children to put the pips and stones in order of size. Use the words 'smaller than', 'bigger than', 'smallest', 'biggest'.
3 Get the children to sort the pips and stones into two sets in a variety of ways, e.g. rough/smooth, shiny/dull, hard/soft. You may get an empty set for some qualities.

Activity H8—Growing pips

Investigating what happens when fruit pips and stones are planted, and when beans of various kinds are put to sprout

You need:
pips and stones from fruits; seeds and beans for sprouting from health food shops and other sources; sprouting jars (see page 143 for advice); cling film; rubber bands; seed compost; labels; a yoghurt carton or small plant pot for sowing seeds for each child.

(For basic information about planting seeds etc. refer to page 141. It takes time for fruit pips and stones to start to grow so you will have to plant them, put them in a suitable place, care for them and be patient. Bean sprouts grow very quickly so you can get 'instant' return from them.)

Warning

This activity involves tasting.
You must emphasise to the children that we only taste things that we know are food. We never taste anything else. They must not taste anything in the classroom unless you tell them to do so. Make sure that the activity is carried out under hygienic conditions – wash hands, use a table cloth, etc.

1 Let each child plant some seeds, pips or stones. Put moist compost in suitable containers and let the children plant their seeds. Then label the pots and cover them with cling film.

seeds,
pips and
stones

seeds

rubber
band

cling film

yoghurt
pot

John

compost

2 Set up jars to grow bean shoots, as described on page 143. Let the children help you to do this and let them take turns to replenish the water. The sprouts appear rapidly and it is soon possible to eat them. Encourage the children to notice which kind of sprouts appear first and what they look like.
3 Let the children find out if the different kinds taste different.
4 Does the taste alter as the sprouts get bigger? When is it best to eat them? N.B. The bigger they are, the more there is to eat but do they taste as good? There is a variety of points which you can discuss with the children depending on their understanding and interest.

Making and doing activities

The problem for the child is:
    'Can you make a bag to carry fruit home from the fruit shop?'

You need:
a variety of fabrics; paper of various strengths; plastic sheet; glue; string; sellotape; staplers; scissors.

For exhibition, have a collection of shop bags of various sizes made from both paper and plastic.

This is approached as a problem solving activity along the lines discussed in the Extensions on page 129. The emphasis throughout is to get the children to think about the problem, to talk about it and produce ideas.

1 The problem   Can you make a bag to carry fruit home from the fruit shop?
2 Exploring the   What characteristics does the bag have to have?
    problem   How big? How strong? Does it have to be waterproof? Does it need handles? What sort of handles?

3 Ideas for solving the problem	What shape might the bag be? What material might be used? What could be used for handles? How can it be stuck together? How can the handles be stuck on?
4 Making	Choosing the best ideas. Selecting construction materials and getting on with the job of making the bag. (The children will need plenty of assistance but at this stage the prime concern is with ideas rather than workmanship! As the children's manual skills develop, increasing regard will be paid to craftsmanship.)
5 Evaluating	Will the bag work? Can you put fruit in it? Are the handles strong enough? Do you think you have chosen your best idea and the best way to make it? (You can now produce your collection of shop bags and you can talk to the children about how they are made and how the makers have overcome the problems which the children no doubt discovered as they tried to make their own bags. You could have produced the shop bags at the ideas stage (3) and, for some problems, this is an appropriate point to produce other people's solutions. In this case, it would probably inhibit the children's own ideas too much.)

Throughout the Making and doing activities, the emphasis is on giving children opportunities, encouragement and motivation to solve problems for themselves, using not only their hands but also their imagination.

Further activities

Some suggestions
1 Make model fruits from play dough, paint them and have a class fruit shop. The children can act out buying and selling.
2 Make a scrap book with a page for each colour and stick in pictures of fruits. Use the book for discussions about where the various items come from, for practice in naming fruits and colours, and for ideas about 'How many?', 'more than', 'less than', etc.
3 Collect fruit colour names, e.g. lemon yellow, tangerine, orange, apple green, tomato red, etc.
4 Try similar activities using vegetables.
5 Use fruits and vegetables for printing.
6 Use cereals and pasta for collage work.
7 Look at which fruits and vegetables are juicy and which are not. Try making drinks from peel and juice where suitable.
8 Mime movements connected with harvesting, e.g. digging, pulling, picking, carrying.

Bonfire night

Language

Mathematics

Physical education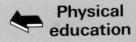

Creative arts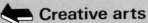

Science

People and their jobs and occupations

Starter Book page 10

Science activities

Making and doing

Teachers' Book page 16

Further activities
Teachers' Book page 18

Introduction

Science activities

The Bonfire night picture provides starting points for Science activities which allow children to investigate aspects of 3D shapes, particularly some of the properties of cylinders and cones. By handling and examining these shapes, children will become better acquainted with their characteristics. Constructing the shapes from layers of plasticine will help the children to appreciate why the cone is a shape which is very stable. The intention is not that the children should understand the reasons for stability but rather that they should begin slowly to be tuned in to ideas which will be developed over many years through varied activities and experiences.

Attention is given to vocabulary describing size, and teachers will no doubt use a variety of means to reinforce and develop the children's oral language.

Eating jacket potatoes (Activity Bo 3) introduces ideas about heat loss and temperature, and about the changes which occur when potatoes are cooked and margarine melts. The final activity concentrates on developing children's listening skills.

Making and doing activities

Two problems for the children are suggested:
   i 'Can you make a model of a Catherine wheel and make it move?'
   ii 'Can you make a drum?'
The first of these activities provides an opportunity to discuss with the children simple ideas about movement and what we have to do to make things move. The second activity allows children to explore the properties and effectiveness of various materials, and to investigate different ways of producing a drum.

Bonfire night   Science activities

Activity Bo1—Cylinders

Observing and investigating the properties of a cylinder

You need:
cylinders of various sizes (with ends) to represent the shape of fireworks; plasticine; rolling pins; various cutters – egg cups, bottle tops, jar lids, etc.

1 Let the children handle the cylinders and talk about them. Find out if they understand the terms 'flat' and 'curved'.
2 Ask if the cylinders are different in any way. If the children say that some are bigger, ask them to describe how they are bigger. Encourage them to use the words 'short', 'shorter than', 'tall', 'taller than', 'long', 'longer than', 'fat', 'fatter than', 'thin', 'thinner than'.
3 Choose a child to stand the cylinders up and put them in height order. Now ask another child to lay them flat and put them in length order.
4 Using the word 'cylinders', ask if they are different in any other way. Encourage the children to look at the thickness and put them in order starting with the fattest.
5 Direct the children's attention now to the end of the cylinder. Tell them that this is a flat surface and ask if they know what the shape of it is called. If they do not know, tell them that it is a circle.
6 They will see that there is another circle at the other end. Ask the children if they think the two circles are the same size and if they can think of a way of finding out.

7 The children can try pressing each end into a piece of flat plasticine or drawing round each circle, cutting it out and placing it over the other circle.

8 Now give each child a ball of plasticine to roll out to 1 cm thickness. (They can roll the plasticine between 1 cm square sticks to give uniform thickness.) Let each of the children use one of the cutters to produce a number of plasticine discs and let them build these into a cylinder.

9 You could follow up this activity by arranging a display of cylinders which we use in everyday life. The children could bring empty containers from home.

Activity Bo2—Cones

Observing and investigating the properties of a cone

You need:
cones of various sizes (to represent fireworks); plasticine; plastic knives

1 Allow the children to handle the shapes and talk about them. Encourage the children to look for the flat surface and the curved surface.
2 They may be able to tell you, without prompting, that one end is fatter than the other.
3 Let them try balancing the cone on its point; ask the children what it reminds them of when it is this way up. They may think of an ice cream, a funnel, a parsnip or a carrot.
4 Now ask the children to look at the fatter end and ask them what shape it is. Place the cone down on its base and ask them what it reminds them of when it is this way up. They may think of a witch's hat, a firework or a traffic cone.
5 Let the children press each end of the cone into a piece of plasticine and compare the shapes which the two ends make.
6 Let the children now use their plasticine to make cones. Then give them plastic knives and suggest that they slice the cones up into discs

7 Ask them what they notice about the circles. Can they put the circles in order of size? Can they put them together again to make a cone once more?

Activity Bo3—Jacket potatoes

Observing and comparing the temperature of jacket potatoes

You need:
use of an oven for about an hour to cook potatoes; each child needs a potato (possibly brought from home) and a teaspoon; three matched potatoes; a raw potato for comparison; margarine to put on the potatoes; a knife; three plates.

Let the children wash the potatoes and put them in the oven to cook for about an hour before you start the activity.

1 When you are ready to start, take the cooked potatoes from the oven. First take the three matched potatoes and put them on separate plates. Leave one whole in its jacket. Cut one in half and put the halves on a plate. Peel the skin off the third and put this on a plate whole. Leave these potatoes on a table while you continue.

2 Cut the children's potatoes in half and put some margarine on each. Also cut the spare potato in half and encourage the children to notice how the cooked potatoes differ from raw potatoes. Let them talk about what is happening to the margarine. (They may complain that it has disappeared!)

3 While they are eating their potatoes, ask them what they think is happening to the three potatoes on the plates. Ask them which they think will be the hottest and which will be the coldest when they have finished eating their potatoes.

4 Cut the two potatoes which are still whole in half and let the children feel each potato and decide which is the hottest and which is the coldest. Let them talk about why they think it happens this way.

Activity Bo 4—Bangs

Observing percussion sounds

You need:
a variety of percussion instruments – drums, tambourines, cymbals; things to bang – saucepans and lids, spoons, metal trays, metal 'thunder' sheet (if possible); sheets of card and paper.

1 Ask the children to describe the sounds which we hear on bonfire night.

2 Show the children various drums, a tambourine and cymbals. Tell them the names of the instruments and then ask the children which will make the loudest bang, like the fireworks.

3 Let the children try each instrument and then decide which is the softest and which is the loudest, and which sounds most like a firework. Let them also try banging the other things which you have collected. Encourage them to talk about the noises and to decide which make the best firework noises and why.

4 Produce a simple rhythm using one of the instruments, and see if the children can clap the rhythm.

Making and doing activities

i   The problem for the child is:
    'Can you make a model of a Catherine wheel and make it move?'

You need:

art straws; cheese boxes; toilet roll and kitchen roll centres; glue;
sellotape; rubber bands; scissors; paper clips; small nails; a hammer.

This problem is divided into two parts: making the firework model, and
making it move. How the children decide to make the firework will
probably depend on the junk materials which you can provide.

The second part of the problem can be approached more systematica[lly]
and will involve discussion with the children along these lines.

1 The problem	Can you make your Catherine wheel move like [a] real one?
2 Exploring the problem	How do real Catherine wheels move? Encourag[e] children to talk about this and to act out how they interpret this movement.
3 Ideas for solving the problem	How can we make things move? The children should be encouraged to think of all sorts of ways of making things move. Discuss with the[m] whether their ideas will solve this particular problem. Let them explore the various means o[f] propulsion which you have provided, e.g. rubb[er] bands. Some children may seek a means of spinning the Catherine wheel, others may want to blow it round (using a straw), and others wi[ll] be happy to push it round or use a rubber band. Whatever means of propulsion they choose, talk to them about the idea that *we* have to provide the 'push' by some means.

| 4 Making | The children should put their ideas into practice as best they can, and they will enjoy doing this. Our interest is in ideas rather than craft skills at this stage. |
| 5 Evaluating | The children can show how their ideas work and talk about which ideas work best. |

Note

This activity is concerned with transfer of energy and enables the children to take a first preliminary step towards an understanding of this subject. It must be emphasised that we are seeking only to draw the children's attention to the idea, no more than that.

In case anyone asks! In real fireworks, propulsion is the result of hot gases being forcibly expelled from the rear of the firework. These gases press on the surrounding air and push the firework forward.

ii The problem for the child is:

'Can you make a drum?'

You need:

various small and big, plastic and metal containers, across the openings of which 'drum' materials can be stretched; plastic sheets of various thicknesses; greaseproof paper; lining paper; brown paper; glue; sellotape; wallpaper paste; rubber bands; string; scissors.

Again, this problem can be approached systematically and the children should be encouraged to talk and discuss the problem.

1 The problem	Can you make a drum?
2 Exploring the problem	What do drums do? What kinds of drums have you used? Did they all make the same sort of noise? What kinds of drums do bands and orchestras have? What decides what kind of noise they make?
3 Ideas for solving the problem	What kinds of drums might you be able to make? What happens when you bang various 'drums' – cake tins or tin cans? Can you alter the sound by putting something inside? If you stretch something across the opening of the tin, is it possible to alter the sound (by varying how tightly the material is stretched)? Which materials make the best noise? Which material do you want to use? How are you going to make your drum?
4 Making	Let the children make and decorate their drums as they think best.

5 Evaluating

The children can demonstrate their drums. Encourage them to talk about the characteristic: of the various drums and let them decide which is best. Perhaps you could finish the activity wit a grand concert.

Note

The tighter the stretch of the material across the mouth of the drum, the higher the pitch. Plastic sheet is easy to pull taut if a strong rubber band i used to hold it in place. Paper is more difficult to tighten but it can be fixed with string or sellotape. Greaseproof paper and brown paper make very satisfactory noise. If lining paper is well brushed with wallpaper paste and left until it is supple, it can be carefully patted into place over the drum opening and left to dry. It is easy to poke fingers through it when it is wet, but as it dries it shrinks and makes a very taut 'skin'.

Further activities

Some suggestions

1 Find out more about what firefighters and park keepers do.
2 Visit a fire station or arrange for the fire engine to visit your school.
3 Arrange to talk to a park keeper or a firefighter.
4 Use the movements of fireworks to stimulate dance or gymnastics.
5 Experiment with paint – splatter, blow, drip, etc. – to get the effect of fireworks.
6 Use dry twigs and tinsel to achieve the effect of sparklers.
7 Bring in some sweet chestnuts with leaves and cases. Roast some chestnuts.
8 Make a guy by stuffing a pair of trousers and a shirt with newspaper. Name body parts and look at ways the guy's body will bend and the child's will not.

What can I do?

Language

Mathematics

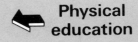
Physical education

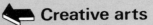
Creative arts

Science

People and their jobs and occupations

Starter Book
page 12

Science activities

Making and doing

Teachers' Book
page 23

Further activities
Teachers' Book page 24

Introduction

Science activities

This topic introduces a number of interesting ideas and activities which the children will enjoy and which will alert them to how our bodies function. Perhaps even more importantly, the children will have an early peep at ideas about force and energy. Obviously, an intellectual understanding of the concepts is a long way off, but these activities prepare the ground.

It is also very important for children to have the opportunity to gain physical experience of forces, and use talk to highlight and explore the experience. It is by talking about them that the children will absorb the ideas.

Making and doing activities

The problem for the child is:

'Can you make a model machine for picking up things?'

Again, it is suggested that you use the structured approach in discussing this problem with the children. It offers scope for imagination and ingenuity; the results at this stage will be rudimentary but the thinking behind the results can be remarkably sophisticated.

What can I do?   Science activities

Activity Wh1—Jumping

Investigating the height and length of jumps; observing some aspects of the force needed

You need:

a space to run and jump; three pairs of wooden skittles of different heights; three light canes (1.5–2.0 m); six small non-slip mats.

1 Ask the children if they can jump. Let them show you. Choose one or two children to jump while the rest watch what happens. What do the feet do? Do they both have to be off the ground at the same time?
2 Ask the children to do little jumps and then big jumps. Can they jump so that nobody can hear them land? Is it easy to do little jumps quietly? Is it easy to do big jumps quietly? Get a few children to try while the others listen; then let the others try.
3 Get out the six wooden skittles. What can the children tell you about them? Can they match them into pairs of the same height? Can they

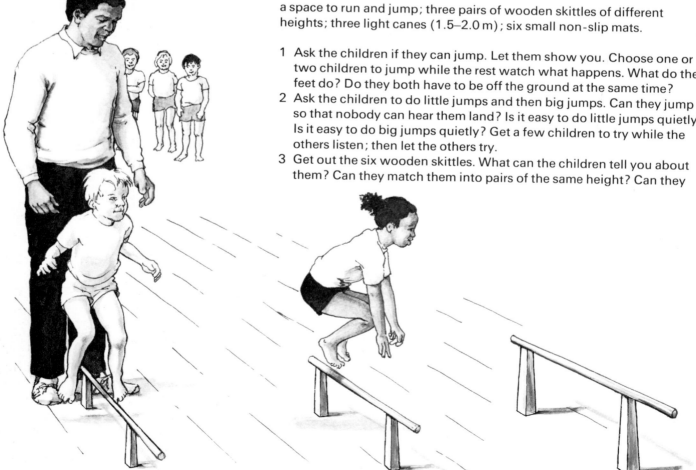

put the pairs of skittles in order of height? Which pair is the shortest? Which pair is the tallest? Arrange the skittles with a cane across each pair. Who can jump over the lowest cane? Who can jump over the next? Who can jump over the highest cane? Which is harder work, jumping over the lowest cane or over the highest? The children may be able to explain this in terms of bumping their feet more or less, or in terms of getting out of breath. Let them discuss both these aspects.

4 Now direct the children's attention to how far they can jump. Get out the six non-slip mats and arrange them so that each pair of mats has a different gap between them. The children may like to imagine that each gap is a river to jump across. Which needs the shortest jump to get

across? Which needs the longest jump? Can they jump across all the gaps? Which gap is the hardest work to cross? What did their feet do?

5 Ask the children who have pets to watch them and see if they can jump.

Activity Wh2—Lifting

Comparing the effort needed to lift buckets with contents of different weights; investigating lifting with legs and feet

You need:
four small buckets with lids (old powder paint buckets are ideal): one should be empty, one filled with polystyrene bits, one with plastic bricks and one with sand.

1 Let the children handle the empty bucket. Is it easy to lift and carry? Would it be easy to lift and carry if it were full?

2 Show the children the three full buckets without lids. Ask one of the children to lift a small amount from each of the buckets and feel its weight in the hand. How heavy does a bit of polystyrene/a plastic brick/a little sand feel? Does one of them feel lighter or heavier than the others or do they all feel about the same? Let the other children try.

3 Do the children think the buckets will be hard or easy to lift? Will they all be the same? Let a child lift one in each hand. Do they feel the same or is one heavier/lighter than the other? Let the child try with a different pair. Is one heavier/lighter than the other? Let the other children try with different pairs, and encourage them to verbalise their experiences using 'heavier than' and 'lighter than'. Ask the children which would make them most tired if they had to carry it a long way.

4 Now put the lids on the buckets and move them around. Ask a child to come and find the sand bucket without looking inside. You can play this game for a short time and then see if they can identify the contents by lifting the buckets with their feet and legs instead of their hands and arms. To do this, let a child sit on a chair and then hook his or her foot under the handle of the bucket. Is it easier with feet or hands?

Activity Wh3—Fingers and toes

Investigating and comparing how good fingers and toes are for picking up things

You need:

for each child: a small ball, a bean bag, a piece of Lego, a 1p piece, a short piece of cotton thread, a fat pencil.

1 Ask the children to tell you about their hands and fingers. How many fingers on one hand? Are they all the same? Which is the longest? Which is the shortest? Where do they bend? How many joints on each finger? How many joints on the thumb?
2 Can the children make all their fingers wiggle together? Can they wiggle one at a time keeping the others still? Which fingers can touch the thumb on the same hand?
3 Now ask each child to take off one shoe and sock and ask them all to look at their feet. How many toes are there? Are they all the same? Which toe is the longest? Which is the shortest? How many joints are there on each toe? Can the children wiggle their toes all at once? Can they wiggle them one at a time? Can the big toe touch any other toes on the same foot?

4 Now give each child a ball, a bean bag, a piece of Lego, a 1p piece, a fat pencil and a piece of cotton thread. Ask them to pick up the ball. How many fingers are they using? Are they using the thumb? Repeat this with the other items. Can the children pick up each item using only the thumb and the index finger? Can they pick up any of the items without using their thumbs?
5 Can the children pick up any of the items with their toes? Can they think of any other parts of the body they could use to pick up some of the things, e.g. elbow joint, chin?
6 Ask children with dogs and cats if they know how their pets pick up things. Why do they not use their paws? Why do we not use our mouths?

Activity Wh4—Faces

Observing and investigating some facial movements

You need:

for each child: a hand mirror, or access to a larger mirror.

1 Ask the children to tell you what features they have on their faces. They can look at their faces in the mirrors as you talk together. How many eyes do we have? What shape are they? What colour? How many noses? How many ears? How many mouths? etc.
2 Play a guessing game: the children have to decide which feature you are describing, e.g. 'It is right in the middle of your face.' 'You have two and they open and close.' 'It is just under your nose,' etc.
3 What can you do with your eyes? Tell the children to keep their heads still and look up, then down, then left and then right. Open eyes wide and then close them tight. Can anyone close one eye and keep the other one open?
4 Can you move your nose at all? Can you move your ears? Can you move your mouth? What shapes can you make with your lips? Will your chin go up and down? Will it go from side to side? Will your tongue go up and down? Will it go from side to side?
5 Make a happy face. Look at your mouth. Make a sad face. What is different? Make a cross face. What has changed? Can you draw a happy face and a sad face?
6 Play a game, 'Guess what my face is saying'. Let the children take turns at expressing various feelings by facial expressions while the rest of the group guesses what the feeling being expressed is.

Making and doing activities

The problem for the child is:
    'Can you make a model machine for picking up things?'

You need:

a selection of junk; glue; string; scissors; paper; pictures of machines which pick up things – cranes, diggers, fork lift trucks, etc.

1 The problem	Can you make a model machine for picking up things?	
2 Exploring the problem	What ways do we have for picking up things? (Grasping with fingers and thumb, gripping, cupping, scooping, etc.) Could you make a model of a machine which would do any of these things?	

A crane

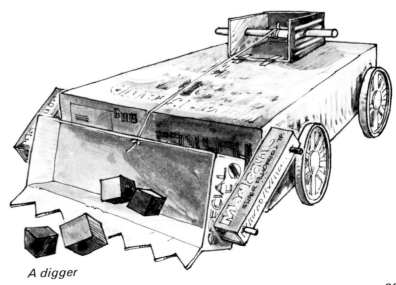

A digger

23

3 Ideas for solving the problem	Let them talk around their ideas. If they lack inspiration, you could produce your collection of pictures to help them. Talk with them about how the various machines work and let the children act out with their hands how the machine picks up things.
4 Making	Let the children make models of whatever kind of pick-up machines they choose.
5 Evaluating	The children can tell each other how their machines would work; you could have a display of their models. Do not expect to have working models at this stage.

Further activities

Some suggestions

1 Bending – look at various joints and find out in which direction they bend.
2 Pushing and pulling – using fingers and hands pushing together and pulling apart various construction toys, e.g. Lego.
3 Time-ordering events – use a song with actions, to the tune of 'Here we go round the mulberry bush'.

    e.g. play with our friends
          go to bed
          eat our lunch
          watch TV
          go to school

Get the children to discuss and put the actions into a time sequence.
4 What makes me tired? e.g. Standing on one leg, hanging by the arms, jumping several times.
5 Let the children try to repeat a sequence of movements.
6 Making sounds with the body – clapping, stamping, variation of sounds with the mouth.
7 Which parts of the body can you balance on?

Christmas

Language

Mathematics

Physical education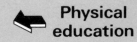

Creative arts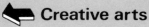

Science

People and their jobs and occupations

Starter Book page 14

Science activities

Making and doing

Teachers' Book page 31

Further activities
Teachers' Book page 33

Introduction

Science activities

The Christmas picture helps to develop children's ability to observe using a combination of senses. Eventually, children should of their own accord bring all the appropriate senses to bear on any observational task. However, care must always be taken to emphasise that tasting is allowed only when it is suggested by the teacher, and only when food is being examined.

The children are able to explore a variety of shapes and materials. The activities are planned so that the steps on the road to scientific competence and understanding are very small. The children should have ample opportunity to explore for themselves and understand things in their own good time.

Some of the activities in this topic reinforce the work of other topics and some expand it. The overall structuring of the activities ensures that skills and understanding develop gradually. For example, the main purpose in Activity C2 is to observe rounded 3D shapes, but children are also encouraged to note the properties of the rubber of the balloon. In Activity C4, the children observe the common properties of the material (metal) from which the bells are made. It will be a very long time before they can be expected to understand fully the properties of materials.

Making and doing activities

Two problems for the children are suggested:
   i 'Can you make a party hat?'
   ii 'Can you make a decoration to hang on the Christmas tree?'
The first of these activities provides children with a real measuring problem and an opportunity to investigate the properties of different kinds of paper. The second activity is concerned with children's creative ideas, and these are tempered by the practicalities of what the branches of a Christmas tree can support.

It should be remembered that Making and doing is intended to introduce children to purposeful, creative, practical activity. It is only a beginning and although a pattern for solving problems is suggested, the main concern is to draw out and develop children's ideas.

Christmas   Science activities

Activity C1—Fairy lights

Observing colours of fairy lights; repeating a sequence

You need:
a set of coloured fairy lights and somewhere to plug them in; a variety of beads matching the colours of the fairy lights; a threading lace for each child.

1 Put the fairy lights in a line on the table and switch them on.
2 Ask the children to name the colours.
3 Let each child find a bead which is the same colour as the first fairy light and thread this on a threading lace.
4 Continue along the line of lights, naming colours and threading matching beads so that each child has a lace with a colour sequence which matches the fairy lights.
5 Switch off the lights and ask the children to pick out and thread coloured beads so that the first sequence of beads is repeated. If their laces are long enough, let them repeat the sequence again.
6 If you feel that they are ready, you could suggest a pattern to them, for example, three blue, one yellow, two green, and ask them to make this pattern with beads on their laces.

Activity C2—Balloons

Sorting balloons by colour and shape; observing curved 3D shapes

You need:
a selection of balloons of different colours and different shapes; a balloon pump; as many sorting circles as you have colours of balloons.

1 Begin by encouraging the children to look at and feel the balloons before they are inflated. What can the children tell you about the material from which the balloons are made? What does it look like? What does it feel like? What can they do with it? (It is best if they postpone trying to blow them up until a little later.)
2 Choose a yellow balloon. Put it in a sorting circle and ask the children to find all the other yellow balloons.
3 Repeat this with each colour. You may have five or six different colour sets, depending on your packet of balloons.
4 Ask the children which set has most and which has least.
5 Suggest that they look for another way in which the balloons are different. Help them to describe the shapes and then to sort them accordingly, using words such as 'long', 'narrow', 'thin', 'short', 'fat'.
6 They will see that, at the moment, the balloons are flat shapes. Ask the children what shape they think the balloons will be when they have air in them. (You could let the children try to blow up their own balloons but it may be better to use the balloon pump.)
7 When each balloon is inflated, ask the children to describe the shape. Let them hold the balloons and feel their curves. The shapes may remind them of some of the fruit observed in the Harvest activities.

Activity C3—Nuts

Sorting nuts by shape and texture

You need:
a selection of nuts: hazelnuts, Brazil nuts, walnuts and almonds — some of each are needed but not more than ten of any one kind; four sorting circles; nutcrackers.

1 Put one nut of each type into a separate sorting circle.
2 Ask the children what the nuts are and find out if the children know the names of the nuts.
3 Now let them sort the remainder of the nuts, putting them in the appropriate circles.

27

4 Ask the children which set has the most. Let them count each set first and then check by putting the largest set in a row and matching the next set to it, one to one.
5 Now give each child in the group one nut of each type, for handling and discussion.
6 Suggest that they feel the nuts and shake them. Let them tell you which ones make a noise when shaken and ask them what is making that noise. You could open one of each kind to show them. Let them see how the nut is packed into its shell.
7 Now ask the children to hold the four nuts behind their backs and to give you the walnut without looking. Repeat this with the other types of nut.
8 Give the children their nuts back and ask each of them to put the hazelnut on one side and to consider the Brazil nut, the walnut and the almond together. Ask them to examine the hazelnut carefully and get them to tell you how it is different from the others. Their first observation will probably be that it is the smallest and they may notice also that it is shiny and the others are dull.
9 Encourage them now to compare how the nuts feel different, using the words 'rough', 'smooth', 'rougher than', 'smoother than'.
10 Your more able children may notice that the hazelnut has no ridges or seams, whereas the other three do. If any of the children do notice this, suggest that they try to count how many parts the surface is divided into.

Activity C4—Bells

Observing the shape and surface appearance of bells; listening for softest and loudest

You need:

a hand bell; a bicycle bell; sleigh bells.

1 Let the children look at the three different kinds of bells and ask them how they are different. Encourage them to look for differences in size and shape, and perhaps in surface appearance.
2 Now ask them if they think that the bells are the same in any way. Let them feel the bells and look more closely at them. They may notice that they are cold, hard and shiny.
3 Ask the children how many circles they can find in each bell.
4 Let the children ring the bells and ask them how they do this.
5 Ask which bell gives the loudest ring and which the softest.

Activity C5—White

Observing white; observing the texture of icing sugar

You need:
icing sugar; a bowl; a spoon; magnifying glasses.

This activity should be carried out when you are about to ice buns or a Christmas cake for the children, or use icing sugar in some other culinary activity, such as sweet-making. Another possibility is to use icing sugar to make a pattern on a plain sponge cake by sprinkling it on a doily placed on the cake.

1 Put a few tablespoonfuls of icing sugar into a bowl. Allow it to fall gradually from the spoon into the bowl and let the children make comments on their observations. Ask them to describe what they see and encourage them to use the words 'powder' and 'white'. Tell them that it is icing sugar.
2 Give the children a small amount in their hands and suggest that they press their hands together. Ask them what has happened to the icing sugar.
3 Now tell the children to rub their hands together and ask them if their hands feel different. Encourage them to use the word 'smooth' here.
4 Suggest that they look carefully at their own hands and at their friends' to see what has happened. (They may like to look more closely at the lines on their hands using a magnifying glass.)
5 Press the back of the spoon into the icing sugar in the bowl, so that the children can see the smoothness as well as feel it.
6 Then use the icing sugar in the way you have chosen.

aking a pattern on a sponge ke with icing sugar

Activity C6—Holly

Observing holly

You need:
some holly with plenty of berries and prickly leaves; plasticine; compost and pots for seed planting.

1 Let the children look closely at the holly and ask them if they know its name.
2 Find out if they can label the parts, i.e. leaf, stem and berry.
3 Now give them each a leaf. Allow them time to talk about their leaves. Establish the colour and suggest that they turn their leaves over. Ask the children how the other side is different. Look for words like 'shiny' and 'dull'.
4 Ask the children if they think both sides are green. Can they describe the difference?
5 Now suggest that they touch the points carefully, and ask them what it feels like.
6 Help them to count the number of points on their leaves. Are all the leaves the same?
7 Ask who has the largest leaf. Is it the leaf with the most points?
8 Suggest that they look at the shiny side. Ask them if the veins remind them of anything.
9 Establish the colour of the berries and ask the children to think of other red things at Christmas.
10 Point out here that the berries are poisonous and that the children must never taste them. You could cut some of the berries so that the children can see the seeds inside. Does each berry have the same number of seeds?
11 Plant some of the berries. (They take a long time to germinate.)
12 The children could press their leaves into plasticine to make an impression.

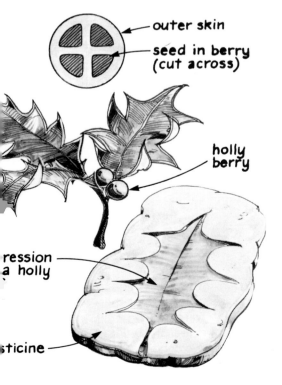
outer skin — seed in berry (cut across) — holly berry — ...ression ...a holly — ...sticine

29

Activity C7—Christmas tree

Observing and sorting Christmas tree baubles by colour, surface and shape

You need:

shiny Christmas tree baubles of various shapes, including spheres of different colours and different sizes; silver foil; glitter; glue; ping pong balls; sorting circles.

1 Let the children handle the decorations and talk about them. Explain that they are fragile and the children must take care.
2 Discuss with the children the various colours and shapes and find out whether the children can tell you if the decorations are the same in any way. If they cannot make the observation that they are all the same in that they are all shiny, ask them instead how they are different and proceed to sort by colour and shape.
3 Now ask the children to give you all the ones which are shaped like a ball. Tell them that these are spherical and put them together with the ping pong balls in one set.
4 Find out if the children can tell you now how the spheres are different. They may detect differences of colour and size first of all, but they should eventually see that the ping pong balls are dull and the others shiny.
5 Let each of the children hold a silver bauble close to their eyes and move it slowly away again. Let them talk about what they see. Suggest that they do the same with the ping pong ball.

Examining and making Christmas tree baubles

6 Ask the children if they can think of a way of using the ping pong ball to make a shiny decoration. Try some of their suggestions and also try wrapping one of the balls in silver foil (pressing it all over to make it smooth) and putting glue over the other and rolling it in glitter.
7 Now let the children examine the two decorations which you have made and compare them. Which one can they see their faces in?

Making and doing activities

i The problem for the child is:
   'Can you make a party hat?'

You need:
coloured tissue paper; sugar paper; crepe paper; glue; scissors; string; a stapler; a large mirror would be useful.

As in earlier activities, children can be encouraged to talk about and discuss their problem along these lines.

1 The problem	Can you make a party hat?
2 Exploring the problem	What is the hat for? How should it look? Does it have to keep you warm? Does it have to keep out the rain? Can you make it fit into a cracker?
3 Ideas for solving the problem	Encourage the children to think of different kinds of hats they might make, including crowns and bag shapes. Let them look at the materials which you have provided and the trimmings they might use. Let them explore the properties of the different kinds of paper. Let them feel the stretch quality of crepe paper and discover how it only stretches in one direction. They can find out how small tissue paper will fold.
4 Making	Having decided the sort of hat they want to make, the children will have to decide how to set about the task. A major problem for them will be how to make it the right size. Let them talk about this and explore different ideas. They may want to use a piece of string for measuring and prefer to work with a partner. Which part of their heads will they have to measure? Which of the partners has the bigger head? How can they tell? (The easiest party hat to make is probably a crown. A strip of paper 70 cm by 20 cm provides an easy start for this.)

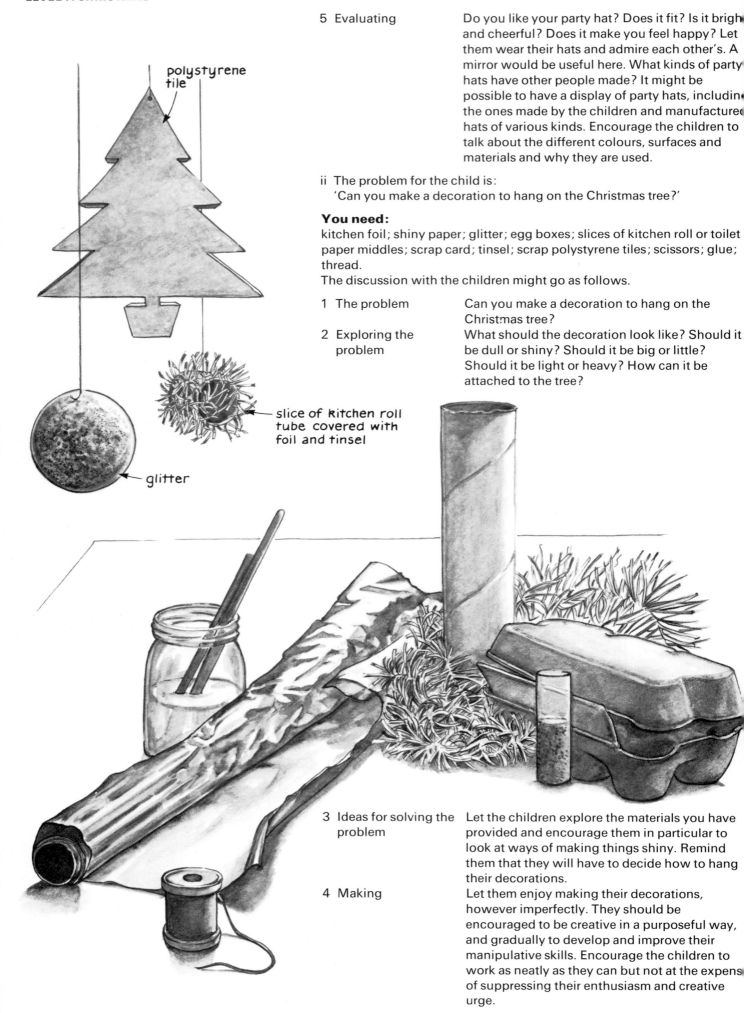

polystyrene tile

slice of kitchen roll tube covered with foil and tinsel

glitter

5 Evaluating

Do you like your party hat? Does it fit? Is it bright and cheerful? Does it make you feel happy? Let them wear their hats and admire each other's. A mirror would be useful here. What kinds of party hats have other people made? It might be possible to have a display of party hats, including the ones made by the children and manufactured hats of various kinds. Encourage the children to talk about the different colours, surfaces and materials and why they are used.

ii The problem for the child is:
   'Can you make a decoration to hang on the Christmas tree?'

You need:

kitchen foil; shiny paper; glitter; egg boxes; slices of kitchen roll or toilet paper middles; scrap card; tinsel; scrap polystyrene tiles; scissors; glue; thread.

The discussion with the children might go as follows.

1 The problem	Can you make a decoration to hang on the Christmas tree?
2 Exploring the problem	What should the decoration look like? Should it be dull or shiny? Should it be big or little? Should it be light or heavy? How can it be attached to the tree?
3 Ideas for solving the problem	Let the children explore the materials you have provided and encourage them in particular to look at ways of making things shiny. Remind them that they will have to decide how to hang their decorations.
4 Making	Let them enjoy making their decorations, however imperfectly. They should be encouraged to be creative in a purposeful way, and gradually to develop and improve their manipulative skills. Encourage the children to work as neatly as they can but not at the expense of suppressing their enthusiasm and creative urge.

5 Evaluating

Do you like what you have made? Is it bright and shiny? Is it too big, too heavy or is it just right? Is it as bright and shiny as the things you buy from the shops? Why are shop things very shiny? (Different specialised materials – mirror glass, coated plastics, etc.)

A Christmas tree decorated with the children's ornaments provides a means of displaying their efforts.

Further activities

Some suggestions
1 Make crackers from pieces of toilet roll middles and coloured paper to hold the party hats which the children have made.
2 Make a display of white things, e.g. cotton wool, icing sugar, milk, flour, paper, etc.
3 Make a collection of pictures of different kinds of bells. Collect as many real bells as possible to make a display. How are the bells the same? How are they different?
4 Compare the leaves of a Christmas tree with holly leaves.
5 Make a collection of leaves of evergreen trees and shrubs.
6 Use a Father Christmas sack as a feely bag.
7 Look at chimneys. What are they for? Do all houses have them? Why do some houses not have them?

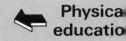

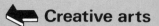

Language

Mathematics

Physical education

Creative arts

Science

People and their jobs and occupations

Starter Book
page 16

Science activities

Making and doing

Teachers' Book
page 40

Further activities
Teachers' Book page 41

Introduction

Science activities

'Clothes' is a very useful topic for introducing observation of texture and for investigating some of the properties of materials. The matching of buttons to garments introduces sorting where more than one property is to be considered, in this case, colour and size. A later activity carries sorting a stage further and provides an opportunity to include purpose as an additional factor.

Very simple ideas about symmetry are explored in looking at children's clothes and the human bodies they fit – back and front, left and right.

Ideas about heat retention are explored and a simple investigation into the effectiveness of using a glove for keeping in heat is described. The last investigation examines the water repellent properties of various materials.

Making and doing activities

The problem for the child is:

'Can you make a rain hat for a doll or teddy bear?'

This activity enables the children to use what they have found out about the water repellent properties of materials in a practical way.

Clothes   Science activities

Activity Cl1 —Buttons

Sorting buttons by size and colour

You need:
coloured buttons giving sets of the same size (e.g. coat size, cardigan size, shirt size – try to avoid intermediate sizes), sets of the same colour, and sets with the same number of holes; sorting trays; small boxes; garments without buttons – an old coat, a cardigan, a shirt.

1 Give the children time to examine the buttons and talk about them freely.
2 Put one button of each colour into a separate sorting compartment and ask the children to put in all the buttons of the same colour and sort by colour in this way. Guide them in the same way to sort by size and by number of holes. Discuss with them what the sorted groups have as a common property.
3 Show the children an item of clothing with buttons and ask them why they think someone chose those particular buttons for that garment. Discuss colour match.
4 Set out your selection of garments with a small box by each one. Ask the children to put buttons to match each garment in the box next to it.
5 When this is done, take one garment and a good selection of buttons of the same colour; ask the children to choose which button would be best. Help the children to consider size. Encourage the children to give reasons for their choice.

Activity Cl2—Feely bag

Observing the texture of clothing materials

You need:
a variety of dolls' clothes of as wide a range of textures as possible; a carrier bag.

1 Ask the children to stroke their jumpers and their shirts. What do they feel like? (smooth, hairy, rough, soft, etc.)

35

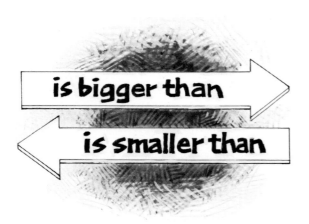

2 Look at the selection of clothes with the children. Take one garment a[t] a time and ask the children how they think it will feel. Will it feel rough/smooth/hairy/scratchy?

3 Choose three garments with very different textures. Show them to the children and then place them out of sight. Tell the children that the clothes are in a shop and they are going to play a shopping game. One child takes the carrier bag to the shop and places one of the garments in it without letting anyone else see which one it is. The chil[d] brings the bag back and holds it high so that the other children have t[o] decide which garment it is by touch. Ask first what it feels like and the[n] ask which garment it is.

4 If children find this easy, try using garments where the texture is similar.

Activity Cl3—Right size

Ordering garments by size and using appropriate vocabulary

You need:

three dolls of different sizes; a set of clothes for each doll (same items in each set); a large cardboard box to hold the clothes; several cardboard arrows, as on the left.

1 Show the children the three sizes of one of the items of dolls' clothing and ask the children to tell you how they are different – size, colour, texture, etc. Ask the children to tell you how they are the same. Get on[e] child to put them in order of size with the biggest on the left. Read the 'is bigger than' arrows with the children and put two of the arrows between the garments.

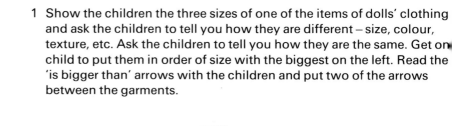

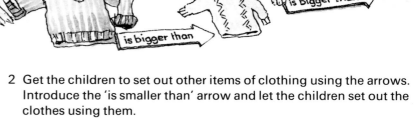

2 Get the children to set out other items of clothing using the arrows. Introduce the 'is smaller than' arrow and let the children set out the clothes using them.

3 Mix all the clothes up in the box and produce the three dolls. Ask the children to dress the dolls in the clothes that fit them. Help them to use 'bigger than', 'smaller than', 'too big', 'too small'.

Activity Cl4—Getting dressed

Sequencing – putting on clothes

You need:

a set of girl's clothes and a set of boy's clothes, including gloves, socks and shoes.

1 Talk about each item of clothing briefly with the children. Ask them to tell you the colour, the texture, whether it is especially for a boy or a girl, whether it fastens and if so how. Make sure all the children can name each garment and the part of the body it fits.

2 Help the children, with much discussion, to set out the clothes in the order they put them on. Use the ordinal numbers: 'We put this on first, this second' etc.

first second third fourth fifth sixth

3 Look at the differences between the front and the back of garments. Ask individual children to put a garment down to see the front and the back of it. Ask the children to describe the difference between the front and the back. Encourage them to notice that the neck opening of a jumper is higher at the back than the front. Discuss with them how the shape of the garment has to be related to the shape of our bodies.
4 Look for twos with the children – two socks, two gloves, two armholes, two sleeves, two trouser legs, two shoes.

Activity CI5—Feet and hands

Investigating symmetry (mirror images) of socks and gloves, feet and hands

You need:
socks and gloves of different textures and colours; black sugar paper; a tray; talcum powder; hair lacquer.

1 Give the children the socks and ask them to find the pairs. Discuss the colours, textures and sizes. Take one pair and ask the children if both socks are exactly the same. Does it matter which feet they go on? Ask the children to draw round a pair of socks with both socks facing the same way and then with them facing in opposite directions. Do socks have a front and a back as gloves do?

2 Get the children to examine their feet. Are they both the same? Which side is the big toe? Is it nearest the door or nearest the window? Is that true for both feet? Use 'left' and 'right' to label feet.

3 Put some talcum powder on the tray and place the black sugar paper so that a child can step from the tray on to the paper. Let a child step barefoot in the talc and then step carefully on to the sugar paper, so that two neat footprints are produced. (These can be fixed by spraying with hair lacquer.)

The footprints can be separated by cutting. Can the children arrange them so that both big toes are on the same side? Can they arrange their own feet so that both big toes are on the outside or both big toes are nearest the door?

4 Go through the same activities with gloves and hands. Name them 'left' and 'right'.

Activity Cl6—Gloves

Investigating whether a glove will keep heat in

You need:

gloves of different kinds – lacy, string, leather, woollen, etc.; two similar screw-topped plastic bottles small enough to fit in gloves; hot water; access to a refrigerator.

1 Let the children examine the gloves, feel them and try them on. Ask them to describe colour, texture, etc. Notice whether the front and back are the same or different. Does each glove fit both hands? Which kind of glove do the children think would be best for keeping their hands warm on a very cold day?

2 Suggest to the children that they try to find out if that glove would be good for keeping something warm. What could they put inside the glove to find out? Will it need to be something that starts off warm or cold? Once you have discussed this point, you can suggest the little hot water bottle.

3 Let the children put the hot water bottle inside the glove and feel the outside of the glove. Ask, 'Can you feel the warmth coming through or not?' 'Can you think of a very cold place to put the glove, to see if it can keep the bottle warm?' Encourage the children to suggest the refrigerator and put the glove in there for about an hour. Point out that you will also have to put a bottle of hot water in the refrigerator without a glove so that you can see what difference the glove makes, if any.

4 When you bring the two bottles out of the refrigerator, let the children feel the bottle without the glove, and put their hands into the glove in which the other bottle has been to see if it has kept the bottle warm. Would this be a good glove to wear on a very cold day? Would it keep your hand warm?

Activity Cl7—Hats

Sorting hats by colour, texture, shape and purpose

You need:

a selection of men's and women's hats – straw, fur, wool, etc. with and without brims: a cap, a balaclava, a sou'wester, a swimming cap, a rain hat and perhaps a riding hat and a crash helmet; sorting circles.

1 Discuss each hat with the children. Who do they think might wear each of the hats? What do they feel like? Why would someone wear each of the hats? What purpose would each of the hats serve? (Take this opportunity to reinforce colour names.)

2 Get the children to sort the hats in various ways, e.g. rough/smooth, hard/soft, with/without brim, man's/woman's.

3 Lead the discussion back to focus on the purpose of the various hats. Ask the children if they can suggest another way of sorting the hats. Help them to carry out their suggestions. If they do not suggest purpose introduce the idea yourself. Make it simple; for example, you could ask what the hats keep out (sun, wind, water) or what they keep in (heat).

Activity Cl8—Waterproof

Investigating which materials are best for keeping out water

You need:
a selection of waterproof items: a plastic mac, a plastic rain hat, an umbrella, a swimming cap, a wellington boot; a few non-waterproof items of clothing; a small watering can; jam jars; rubber bands; sorting circles.

1 Let the children feel the clothes and sort them into those we wear to keep out water and those which will not keep out water. Ask the children to tell you why they think that these items of clothing will keep out the water. Their answers will help you to judge their level of thinking about this.
2 Suggest that the children try sprinkling water on the clothes to see what happens. What happens to the water? Where does it go? Let them sprinkle both the waterproof and non-waterproof clothing and make sure that they notice that the water runs off some materials and soaks into others.
3 Ask the children how they could find out whether any water goes through the various items of clothing. Accept fairly crude solutions, such as putting something dry inside, pouring water on the clothing and then feeling the thing inside to see if it has got wet. For many children, this will be sufficient.
4 To show the children how to refine this test further, where appropriate, fasten part of each garment over a jam jar with a rubber band. Let the children pour a cupful of water on to each of them and compare jam jars to see which lets most water through and which does it most quickly. Which would be the best garment for a wet day and which would be the worst?

plastic mac

cotton blouse

water

cardigan

39

Making and doing activities

The problem for the child is:
'Can you make a rain hat for a doll or teddy bear?'

You need:
a selection of materials including plastic carrier bags, sheets of paper and pieces of non-waterproof fabric; yoghurt cartons; scissors; glue; a stapler.

This problem can be approached systematically and the children should be encouraged to talk about it and discuss their ideas.

1 The problem	Can you make a rain hat for a doll or teddy bear?
2 Exploring the problem	What must a rain hat do? How will you decide which material to use? Could you find out which would be a good material for keeping out the rain? How will you decide what size to make the hat? (The children will probably vary enormously in their ability to respond to this problem. The emphasis should be on encouraging their ideas and helping them to tackle the problem at their own level.)
3 Ideas for solving the problem	The children will have to think what shape the hat might be, how big it must be, how it will stay on, and how to make it look nice.
4 Making	The skills which the children display will cover a wide range, and the problem provides plenty of opportunity for helping them develop manual skills.

5 Evaluating	Does the hat fit? Will it keep out the rain? Is it made of the best material? Do you like it?

Further activities

Some suggestions

1 Ask the children to think of clothes that come in pairs. Give them paper and a mirror. Can they draw one of the pair and use the mirror to make the other?

2 Ask the children to draw a jumper. Draw a line down the middle. Colour one side red and the other blue. Can they use the mirror to make a blue jumper and then a red jumper? Draw another jumper. Draw a line across the middle. Colour the top half red and the bottom half blue. Can they use a mirror to make a red jumper and then a blue jumper? Why not?

3 Get the children to draw round both their hands with their fingers spread out. Let them colour each finger on the left hand outline a different colour. Can they colour the right hand outline to make it a pair with the left hand?

4 Puppets: dress these with appropriate clothes for particular characters, e.g. clown, king.

5 Collect pictures of people who wear a uniform. Ask children to bring in sets of play clothes which are uniforms.

6 Look at the differences between summer clothes and winter clothes.

7 Show the children an item of clothing and ask them to mime what they would be doing if they were wearing that clothing, e.g. swimming trunks, football shorts.

Winter

Language

Mathematics

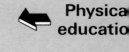
Physical education

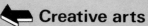
Creative arts

Science

People and their jobs and occupations
Starter Book page 18

Science activities

Making and doing
Teachers' Book page 47

Further activities
Teachers' Book page 47

Introduction

Science activities

The Winter science activities enable children to use their developing abilities to observe and investigate. The first three activities are weather dependent so you will need to take advantage of suitable days. Activity W3 allows children to investigate the floating properties of ice. This will possibly draw to your attention the difficulty which children experience in accepting experimental evidence which does not match up to their instinctive beliefs. They will probably find it difficult to believe that ice will float however big the piece is. Their understanding should not be hurried; they should have many opportunities to observe the evidence and slowly to come to accept and understand it. Each child has to work it out individually. They should be given every encouragement to discuss their observations and their interpretation of that evidence, but only they themselves can develop understanding.

Making and doing activities

The problem for the child is:
   'Can you make a model snow mover for clearing snow off the road?'
This activity for Winter again gives children an opportunity to be imaginative and use their inventiveness in using junk materials to interpret their ideas.

Winter   Science activities

Activity W1—Shadows

Investigating shadows

You need:
a sunny day; fairly large rigid 2D shapes (30–40 cm minimum): square, triangle and circle; large sheets of paper; pencils.

1 Take the children outside and play some games with shadows. Ask the children if they can run away from their shadows. Can they make them longer or shorter? Can they make them look as if they only have one leg? Let the children play and talk about their shadows, in particular about the shape and size of them.
2 Find a place indoors where the sun shines on to the floor. Let one child stand so that his or her shadow can be seen. Ask the children whether they think the shadow is the same size as its owner. Place a large sheet of paper on the floor so that the child's shadow falls on it. The children can then draw round the outline of the shadow.

3 Next, produce the square and suggest the children find out about its shadow. Arrange a table so that the square can be held in the sun and its shadow falls on a sheet of paper on the table. Let one of the children draw round the shadow of the square. The shape of the square and its shadow can then be compared. Is the shadow longer or shorter than the square? N.B. The square should be held so that it is at right angles to the sunlight and is vertical.

4 Investigate the shadows of the triangle and the circle in a similar way.

Activity W2—Snow

Observing and investigating the nature of snow

You need:

a recent fall of snow; a few clean jam jars; a foam bath mat or similar sheet of foam at least 2 cm thick.

1 Take the children out to look at the snow. Get them to tell you all they can about it. What colour is it? Does it feel light or heavy? Is it hard or soft? Is it cold or warm?

2 Ask the children what happens when they tread on a fresh patch of snow. They may be able to tell you that their feet sink into it. Ask what happens to the snow. Does it move away? Does it get squashed together? Does it stay down or come up again? Let them try walking on the piece of foam. Is that like walking on snow or is it different? How is it different? How is it similar?

3 Let the children look at footprints. (You may have to arrange some examples beforehand.) Can the children tell you who might have made the footprints? Were they made by grown-ups or by children? Which way were they going? How can we tell? Let the children make their own footprints and compare them with those of other people. How are they different? Can they tell which child made the footprints without actually seeing the footprints being made?

4 Let each child hold a little snow. What happens to it? What happens to snow when we take it indoors? Suggest that the children fill the jam jars with snow and take them into the classroom to find out. Use the opportunity to explore the idea of fullness: make sure that the children know that the jars are full to the top with snow.

    The children can observe the jars at fairly regular intervals to see what happens. Where does the water appear? Once the snow has melted completely, let the children look at the water. Are the jars full to the top? Which took up more space, the snow or the water? What colour was the snow? What colour is the water? Do the children think that the water is clean?

Activity W3—Ice

Observing and investigating the nature of ice

You need:

a day of keen frost; access to frozen puddles (or you can put out washing-up bowls containing water to produce frozen puddles); a bowl or bucket of cold water; some jam jars; large pieces of ice of various shapes and sizes (you can make ice blocks by putting water in plastic containers and either placing them outside if the weather is cold enough or in a freezer).

1 Take the children out to look at some frozen puddles or the plastic bowls of frozen water. Let the children tell you all they can about how the ice has formed on the water. You may be able to get them to say that the ice is cold and slippery, that it will crack if you tread on it, and that it may have water underneath.

2 Let the children crack the ice and pick up the pieces. Is it warm or cold? Look at the edges. Are they sharp, straight or curved? What is happening to the ice as it is being handled? Ask the children what it is doing to their hands.

3 Take some of the ice indoors and have ready also the blocks of ice which you have prepared. Ask the children what they think will happen if they drop the ice into a bowl of water. Will it float or sink? Before they try it, ask them if they can remember what happens when ice cubes are put into orange squash. Do they float on the top or sink to the bottom? Ask the children about the puddle. Was the ice on the top or at the bottom? Now let them find out whether the pieces of ice which they have brought in will sink or float in the water. Produce the pieces of ice of different shapes and sizes which you have prepared and ask the children to tell you which they think will float and which will sink. Encourage them to give their reasons and respond to these. For example, if a child says a piece of ice will float because it is small, produce a big piece and ask the child about that piece. If a child says the ice floats because it is flat, produce a lumpy piece and ask about that piece. Explore their ideas and try to give them the evidence which suggests that ice floats because of the nature of the ice itself. (You may think that they have grasped the idea at this point but the children will undoubtedly return many times to the idea that little pieces float and big pieces sink. For your information, water is made up of very small particles (water molecules) which in liquid water move about quite freely. In solid water (ice), the particles form a structure rather like three dimensional wire netting. This structure spreads out the particles and makes ice less dense than water. The result is that the less dense ice floats on the more dense water.)

4 Put the other pieces of ice into the jam jars and let the children look at the water which appears. What has happened to the ice? Does the water look clean? (Whether it is clean will depend on the surroundings and how long the ice has been exposed to atmospheric pollution.)

45

Activity W4—Toast

Observing change – when bread is toasted

You need:

an electric toaster; some knives; one pot or metal plate; a plate for each child (this can be paper); a white sliced loaf; some margarine.
N.B. Tasting warning in paragraph 2.

1 Tell the children that they are going to handle food so they must was their hands. Let the children examine the slices of white bread. What colour is it? Is it hard or soft? What happens if it is stroked gently? What happens if it is squeezed between finger and thumb? Does it st squashed or does it spring back?

2 Give each of the children a small piece of bread to spread with margarine. Is it easy to do this? What happens? What does the margarine look like? What colour is it? Does it cover the bread? Let t children eat their pieces of bread, reminding them that it is all right to do so because it is food and you, the teacher, have told them to do so Remind them never to eat or taste anything unless they know it is foc and you have told them they can eat it. Ask the children what kind of noise chewing bread makes.

3 Take two slices of bread, put them on a sheet of paper and draw rour them. Set the toaster for medium browning and put in the two slices bread. Ask the children how they think the toaster turns the bread int toast. They can look into the toaster from above as long as you make sure that they do not get too near. They will be able to see the red ho element. Ask them what colour it is. Does it remind them of anything else? Can they see anything coming out of the toaster? Hold a pot or metal plate above the toaster for a few seconds and let the children examine it. They will see moisture on it. Where did this come from?

4 When the toast is removed from the toaster, steam will be clearly visible, although the children may not recognise it as such. Put the toast on the pot or metal plate for a few seconds and then lift it up so that the children can see the moisture which appears on the plate. What do they think it is? Where has it come from?

5 Put the slices of toast on the outlines of the pieces of bread. What ha happened? Why?

6 Give each child a small piece of toast to examine. Ask the same questions as you did when they were examining the piece of bread.

7 Let each child spread margarine on a piece of hot toast. Is it easy to d this? What happens? What does the margarine look like? What has happened to the margarine? Why? What noise does the knife make? What noise does the toast make when it is chewed?

8 Put a slice of fresh bread on to a piece of paper and draw round it. Pu the bread in a warm place and leave it. Let the children look at it later What has happened? Why?

Making and doing activities

The problem for the child is:
'Can you make a model snow mover for clearing snow off the road?'

You need:
junk of all kinds; glue; scissors.

1 The problem	Can you make a model snow mover?
2 Exploring the problem	What will the snow mover have to do? What is snow like? How can you move it, squash it, melt it, push it out of the way, vacuum clean it up? What are the snags? (For this problem, it may be useful to explore with the children the ways which are used for snow clearing: with a snow plough or with a snow blower. Simpler ways such as shovelling, using a shovel as a mini-snow plough, can also be discussed and experimented with if possible.)
3 Ideas for solving the problem	When the children have explored the problem in their own way, encourage them to decide what kind of snow mover they want to make.
4 Making	At this stage, the role of the teacher is to help the children to find materials which will enable their ideas to be realised. Discuss with the children the properties of the materials they are using – shapes of containers, materials from which they are made, how good the glue is.
5 Evaluating	In this instance, let the children talk to everyone else about the models they have made. You could organise an exhibition in conjunction with a wider project about life in snowy countries.

Further activities

Some suggestions

1 Talk about sliding on ice and snow and how we enjoy it. If possible, make a display of equipment used for sliding on ice and snow, e.g. ice skates, sledge, skis. Get the children to look at the part which touches the snow or ice. They should notice that the contact surface is narrow, hard and smooth. N.B. Care must be taken with skates – they can be very sharp. Collect pictures of winter sports and make a scrap book.

2 Talk about the times when we do not want to slide on ice or snow. How do we stop ourselves sliding? Look at the soles of shoes and the treads of car and bicycle tyres. Use shoe soles, bicycle tyres and car tyres to make prints on a huge sheet of paper. Can the children recognise dog tracks and bird tracks?

3 Make ice lollies with different flavourings of different colours. Notice the patterns in the ice. Where else do we sometimes see icy patterns?
Let the children taste the ice lolly mixture before it is frozen. Does freezing alter its taste? (The taste will be dulled.) Add colouring to produce a range with the same flavour but different colours. Does the colour alter the taste? Can the children tell from the taste what colour the lolly is?

4 Try out slow and fast movements. Which help to get our bodies warm?

5 Look at bare twigs. Do blow patterns with straws using black paint on white paper to look like bare twigs.

6 Act out a winter sports scene using sliding, skating and skiing movements.

LEVEL 2: TOPICS

Spring

The bathroom

The cook

The caretaker

School holidays

INTRODUCTION TO LEVEL 2

The children coming to level 2 activities will already be beginning to establish habits and attitudes which will lead them of their own accord to be curious and to question. They will be developing skills which will enable them to direct their curiosity into action – particularly to use observation skills in a purposeful way. They should be able to understand that the different senses provide them with different information, all of which is useful, and that by selecting which senses they use, they can obtain the most relevant information.

The children will increasingly be involved in investigations and this involvement will develop not only as a consequence of their mental maturation but also as a result of their improving manual skills. Another development should be a growing questioning of what is being discovered and observed, and a looking for reasons. In many cases, the reasons suggested may be unexpected: children can only observe against a background of their own experience. Nevertheless, the reasons are the children's own within their own frameworks and it is on those that we must build.

In level 2, we begin to look at the way in which people use science in all sorts of ways in their jobs and in their everyday lives. The assistant in the florist's shop needs to know about flowers and plants. The caretaker needs to know about cleaning materials. If we are going to sit on the beach, it is useful to have discovered that it is likely to be drier where there are pebbles than where there is sand.

We have tried by means of the prompts to set your mind to thinking about the many instances where science is used. Science and thinking 'scientifically' play a greater part in our lives than we often realise. *Longman Scienceworld* aims to make children more aware of this, and to enable them to use their science confidently and fruitfully.

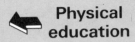
Spring

Language

Mathematics

Physical education

Creative arts

Science

People and their jobs and occupations
Starter Book page 20

Science activities

Starting points	*Starter Book* page	20
Activities	*Teachers' Book*	52

S1 Bulbs   52
Observing and investigating bulbs

S2 Bird cake   53
Observing melting and solidifying – lard

S3 Artificial flowers   54
Observing living and non-living – real and artificial flowers

S4 Green   55
Observing shades of green

S5 Seeds   55
Observing and investigating what happens when seeds are planted

S6 Compost   56
Investigating the composition of potting compost

Making and doing
Teachers' Book page 57

Further activities
Teachers' Book page 58

Introduction

Science activities

Spring is a topic in which every child delights, and some familiar ideas and some less familiar ones are included. What makes a study 'science' for small children depends on questions the teacher asks and how the attention of the children is directed. Just as important is encouraging the children to talk and discuss among themselves what they are observing, doing and thinking. Eavesdropping on such discussions provides many clues about what to do or say next.

In this topic, the children are using their developing skills to study more complex concepts, in particular, melting and living and non-living. It will be interesting to see whether your children think that melted lard is still lard or whether they think that the lard has become water. Living and non-living is another concept which takes time to grasp. Do pebbles grow? Ask your children what they think. Maybe you could set up an investigation to find out.

Making and doing activities

The problem for the child is:

'Can you make a plant pot for one of your seedlings?'

This will also give children an opportunity to explore the properties of another interesting material: clay. The main concern here is to help children to tackle problems with imagination and to develop gradually an understanding of how to set about solving a problem and evaluating the results. The Making and doing section has been written in a disciplined, structured way so that a familiar framework in which to work is established and can be developed as the children progress.

Spring Science activities

Activity S1 — Bulbs

Observing and investigating bulbs

You need:

three hyacinth bulbs complete with roots and leaves (and possibly flowers, but these are not needed for this activity); a knife. (Hyacinth bulbs are rather expensive but it is intended at a later stage to look at onions and to make comparisons with hyacinths.)

1 Let the children examine the complete plants and name the parts: roots, bulb, leaves, stem, flowers. Ask the children to tell you the colour and shape of the leaves. They should be able to say that the leaves are light green at the bottom and dark green at the top and that they are narrow and pointed. Help them to notice this and to develop the appropriate vocabulary.

2 What else can the children tell you about these leaves? Suggest that the children run their fingers gently up and down the leaves and from side to side. What can they feel? Can they feel the ridges? Can they see the ridges? Do the ridges run up and down the leaves or across them? Which direction do the leaves grow in? (Upwards.)

3 Draw the attention of the children to the bulb. Ask them about shape and colour together, and then about the texture. What can the children see at the top of the bulb? What shape is the part that the root grows from? What grows above the bulb? What grows below the bulb?

4 Ask the children to describe the shape and colour of the roots and tell you in which direction they grow. What do the roots do? What are they for?

5 What do the children think might be inside the bulb? Let them try to guess. Ask for suggestions as to how you might find out. The children

might suggest peeling off one layer at a time or cutting it in half either downwards or across the middle. All three approaches are useful. Take one bulb and let the children, one at a time, each remove a layer. Encourage them to examine the pieces as well as the bulb. The children should notice that the bulb becomes very shiny. The pieces have a white part and a thin transparent skin. Soon the pieces become very wet. Let the children rub their fingers together with the moisture on them. How does it feel? Sticky? Slippery? Getting to the centre of the bulb may take some time and, while this is continuing, you could cut the other two bulbs, one vertically and the other horizontally.

6 What patterns do the children see? What do they think the lines or rings are? Do the leaves come from inside the bulb? What is the same about the bottom of the leaves and the other layers of the bulb?

7 Remind the children to wash their hands at the end of this activity.

Activity S2—Bird cake

Observing melting and solidifying – lard

You need:
peanuts in shells; maize; sunflower seeds; apple pieces; sultanas; biscuits; stale cake; lard; a glass pan; two bowls – at least one of them transparent; a spoon; a heat source.

1 Let the children examine the peanuts in their shells. Ask them to tell you two things about them, e.g. they are light brown, and they rattle when you shake them. Ask the children to find out which is the best place to press them to open them. Let them explore this freely. Do they discover that the nut shells are like pea pods with 'seams' down the sides? Let them shell the nuts and place them in the opaque bowl.

2 Now give the children the maize and the sunflower seeds. Can they tell you two things about each of them? Ask the children for differences and similarities. Put these seeds in the bowl with the nuts.

3 Continue to ask for observations in twos: for the apple pieces and the sultanas, and the cake and the biscuits. Help the children to notice shape, colour, smell, pattern, etc. Add all these ingredients to the ones in the bowl.

4 Show the children the block of lard. Ask what colour and shape it is. Put the lard into the pan and tilt the pan slightly. Ask the children whether the lard moves and whether its shape changes.

5 Now melt the lard over a low heat. Ask the children to describe what is happening. Which part of the lard melts first? Why do they think it happens that way?

6 Pour some of the lard into the transparent bowl. What colour and shape is the lard now? What happens when we tip the bowl? Does the lard move? What does it look like? What does it behave like? (Water.) What do they think would happen if it was just left to cool down? Shall we keep a little and find out?

7 Pour most of the melted lard on to the bird cake mixture and let the children take turns at stirring it. (Keep a little of the melted lard and put it on one side to cool.) What happens to the cake and the biscuit when they mix with the melted lard? Does the same thing happen with the other ingredients?

8 Look at the lard which was left in the bowl. What is happening to it? Is this what the children expected? When the lard has become solid again, ask the children to tell you what has changed. Tip the bowl and ask, 'Does it move?' 'Does it change shape?' 'Does it still behave like water?'

9 When the bird cake has set, scoop it from the bowl. Ask the children what has happened to it. Put the bird cake in a place safe from cats where it can be seen by the children from the window and they can enjoy some bird spotting. What kinds of birds come? Which are there most of? Which ones fight? Do the birds pick their favourite bits out of the cake or do they like it all?

Activity S3—Artificial flowers

Observing living and non-living – real and artificial flowers

You need:
some dried flowers; some real fresh flowers (or a flower) and a matching artificial flower – some realistic imitations can be found; a real plant and its artificial counterpart.

1 Bring into the classroom your real, dried and artificial flowers and you real and artificial plants. Let the children look at them and discuss them.
2 Take your real flower and its artificial counterpart and ask the children to describe each of them, referring to colour, shape, size, texture, smel weight and any other feature that they may notice. Ask them now how the two are the same and how they are different.

3 Ask the children if there are any other differences which they could no tell simply from observing. Where did the two flowers come from? Wh made them? What will happen to them if we keep them? Should they be kept until tomorrow to see what happens? (Do not put the real flower in water at this point unless someone suggests it. If someone does, ask why and see if the child wants you to put the artificial flowe in water as well. If he or she says this is not necessary, ask why not. If no-one is concerned about the water, keep an eye on the flower and when it looks droopy, point this out to the children. Ask what is happening to it and what needs to be done.) Keep the real flower and the artificial flower together and show that eventually the real flower dies, but the artificial flower does not alter and it does not matter whether or not it is in water.
4 Now produce the dried flowers and let the children examine these. How are they different from the fresh flowers and how are they different from the artificial flowers? Where do they come from? Who made them? Are they alive or are they not alive? What do they need t keep them as they are? (There is a host of questions which may be asked. It is an intriguing subject which will cause much discussion ar speculation.)

5 Put the real and artificial plants side by side and get the children to describe them and talk about them as they did about the flowers. Ask them again how the two are the same and how they are different.

6 What is different about the plants which you cannot tell simply by observing them? What will they look like next week? Will they still look exactly the same as they are now or will they look different? Keep the plants side by side and discuss whether there is a need for water for the plants. Help the children to see that the real plant does need water but the artificial plant does not. Let them see also that the real plant grows. (It is to be hoped that the plant does grow and does not die, but the point that real plants do die needs to be demonstrated somehow.)

   Take any opportunity to let the children observe that living things change and that they have essential needs and functions.

Activity S4—Green

Observing shades of green

You need:

to take the children for a walk; a selection of magazines; glue and glue spreaders; scissors and a piece of light green sugar paper for each child; a tray.

1 Take the children for a walk near your school and ask them to look for anything which is green. Get them to distinguish between living, growing things and things which people have made or painted. Talk to them about all the different shades of green. (If you can arrange for your walk to be in a park or garden when the new leaves are beginning to appear, this is particularly valuable.)

2 Back in the classroom, give the children some magazines and ask the children to look for green things in them. Let the children cut out all the green things and put the pieces in a tray.

3 When you have a reasonable collection of green pieces, give each child a piece of light green sugar paper. Ask the children what colour it is and establish that it is light green. Let them select green pieces from the tray and talk about the colour, and whether the pieces are all one colour or whether they are shaded.

4 Let the children choose five or six green pieces each and arrange these as a collage on their sugar paper. When they are satisfied with the arrangement, they can stick the pieces down and you can make a green display.

Activity S5—Seeds

Observing and investigating what happens when seeds are planted

You need:

a packet of French marigold seeds; a packet of nasturtium seeds; a packet of lobelia or other very fine seeds (not pelleted); John Innes seed compost (or similar); a paper or plastic cup for each child; a small watering can; a tray; cling film; a magnifying glass; pieces of white paper. (See note about types of compost on page 141.)

1 Let the children look at the packets of seeds. What are they called? What colour will the flowers be? How tall should they grow? The information on the packet may be in feet and inches. Show the children on a ruler what this will be in centimetres. You can stand the ruler on the floor and ask the children whether the plants will grow past the tops of their shoes, past the tops of their socks, or past their knees.

2 Let the children feel the packets and guess whether the seeds are big or little. Let the children open the packets carefully and sprinkle a few of each kind of seed on to a piece of white paper. Write the names of the seeds on the paper.

French marigold

3 Now let the children examine the seeds. A magnifying glass is useful here. The children should be able to make comparisons of shape, colour, size, texture, etc. The French marigold seeds are very interesting with their feathery ends.

4 Look at the nasturtium seeds and notice variations in size, colour and shape. Can the children pick out the smallest, the biggest, the darkest, the lightest, the roughest, and the smoothest seeds?

5 Ask the children what seeds are. What do they do? Will they grow if left on the paper? What should be done to make them grow? Look at one of the packets again and read to the children what it says about planting the seeds. Do the children know the word 'sowing'? What is compost?

6 Produce the compost and let the children feel it. Is it dry or wet? Introduce the word 'moist'. Give each child a paper or plastic cup with a few holes in the bottom. Let them fill their cups with compost and choose which kind of seeds they would like to plant. Read the instructions on the packet and let the children plant their seeds. Label each cup with the type of seed and the child's name. Place the cups on a tray and let one of the children water them lightly. A covering of cling film will help stop them drying out.

7 Make a simple calendar so that the children can cross off the days and know when to start looking for the seedlings. (The packets will give you an idea how many days it is likely to be before the seeds germinate.)

e.g. Wednesday   We planted our seeds
      Thursday   day 1 . . . . .
      Friday   day 2 . . . . .
             and so on
      Thursday   day 8 We can start looking for . . . etc.

Activity S6—Compost

Investigating the composition of potting compost

You need:

a small white mixing bowl; some pint-size plastic beer glasses; white kitchen paper towel; John Innes compost or similar (not a peat based compost); magnifying glasses; pieces of white paper; small sticks for stirring; teaspoons; labels (see 4).

1 Put some of the compost into the mixing bowl. Ask the children if they can remember what it is. Let them put their fingers in it and stir it round. What does it feel like? Does it feel rough or smooth? What noise does it make on the bottom of the bowl? Are all the pieces the same size?

2 Give each child a piece of white paper to put on the table. Pour out a small amount of compost for each child. Tell the children that they are going to be detectives and look for any interesting things which they can find in the compost. Let them use magnifying glasses and help them to notice fibres, bits of sticks, and also tiny pebbles and stones of various colours – some rounded, some sharp. Which bits might have made the scratchy noise in the bowl?

3 What happens when compost is put in water? Produce the plastic glasses and let the children half-fill these with water. Ask the children if they think that the compost will float or sink if they put some in the water. Let them add about two teaspoonfuls of compost to their glasses of water and then give the mixture a gentle stir. What happens when it settles? The children should be able to see that some of the compost floats and some sinks to the bottom. What size are the pieces that float? Do some big pieces float? Do some tiny pieces float? Which bits are the ones that are floating? Which bits sink? Are there any big pieces that have sunk? Are there little pieces which have sunk?

4 Let the children carefully spoon the floating pieces off the surface and put them on to a piece of kitchen towel. Give each child a label with 'These pieces floated' to place alongside. Now show them how to pour off the water gently from the glass, leaving the sediment at the bottom. Let the children scrape this out on to pieces of kitchen towel and give them labels with 'These pieces sank'.

5 Let the children look carefully at the material which sank and that which floated. What happened to the sticks and fibres? What happened to the small stones and pebbles? What does it feel like if they rub the material that floated between their fingers? What does the material which sank feel like? How do they feel different?

Making and doing activities

The problem for the child is:
    'Can you make a plant pot for one of your seedlings?'

You need:
a selection of plant pots (as examples of types); junk materials; clay – either for firing or a non-firing variety, as appropriate.

Encourage the children to approach the problem along the following lines.

1 The problem	Can you make a plant pot for one of your seedlings?
2 Exploring the problem	What does a plant pot have to do? What does the material from which it is made have to do? What about water? What kind of conditions will the seedling need to grow? Where will the pot stand? What should it look like?
3 Ideas for solving the problem	Probably, the children's ideas are going to be determined very largely by the materials which you provide for making the pot. Help them by providing examples of pots made from a variety of materials but concentrate on the idea of clay pots.

4 Making

Show them how to mould a thumb pot. Talk to them about the size it needs to be and the need for a drainage hole. Show them how the damp clay can be decorated by scratching etc. and how the dried clay can be painted.

Use every opportunity to talk about the properties of the clay and the way in which the properties change as the clay dries. (The children could also make a small saucer for the pot to rest on.)

5 Evaluating

Does the pot stand up? Is it the right size? Does the drainage hole work? Does the saucer hold the pot? Does it hold the drainage water? Does the pot look nice?

You can have an exhibition of the finished pots and, eventually, a flower show!

Further activities

Some suggestions

1 Plant some of the seeds used in the bird cake, e.g. peanuts (plant the pod whole for maximum interest), sunflower seeds, apple pips.
2 Ask a florist to come into school to talk about her or his job and show the children some of the ways in which flowers can be displayed etc.
3 Invite somebody from the local flower arrangers' club to visit the school.
4 Let the children make a green 'spectrum'. Give each child a strip of paper about 6 cm × 30 cm. Ask the children to put a lot of yellow paint in one section of their paint palettes and to start off by painting a yellow stripe at the left hand end of their paper. Then get them to add a little blue to the yellow paint and then paint another stripe, and so on until they have a very bluish green.
5 Get a decorator's paint card of greens and let the children look at the names. Why might these names have been chosen? What names for greens do the children know? Can they suggest a name for one of their stripes?
6 Collect pictures of parent and baby animals to name and match.
7 Movement – growing slowly from a curled-up tight position to a stretched position.

The bathroom

 Language

 Mathematics

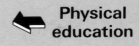 Physical education

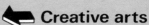 Creative arts

Science

Introduction

Science activities

The bathroom topic provides the setting for a range of activities which enhance and reinforce the development of the skills of observing, sorting and investigating. With observing, the children should eventually be able to decide for themselves what to observe, and beyond that to determine which observations are significant in a particular investigation. At this stage, however, the children still need a lot of guidance. In the activities in level 1, much of the observation used one or two of the senses, and these were specified. Now, more instances are introduced where observation requires all the senses to be involved. The investigations of the nature of solids and liquids provide a good illustration of this.

The children are also invited in one of the activities (Activity B6, Steamed up) to make a prediction. This is not a prediction in the orthodox scientific sense but it is more than a blind guess. Perhaps it is best to consider it to be a sensible suggestion based on reasons which are valid for the child. This same activity also demonstrates the gradual introduction of more sophisticated concepts – in this case, condensation. However, there is no need to introduce the word at this stage unless it seems to be useful to the children.

Making and doing activities

The problem for the child is:

'Can you make a boat from a matchbox tray which you can play with in the bath? Can you make it so that it will carry a cargo of six 1p pieces?' This activity will provide children with opportunities to apply their developing understanding of floating and sinking and to consider the useful properties of some of the materials which they have investigated.

The bathroom   Science activities

Activity B1 — Dolls

Observing similarities and differences between dolls and between dolls and a baby; the order of putting on dolls' clothes

You need:
a water tray preferably on a stand; a jug of cold water; a jug of steaming hot water; some soap; for each child a waterproof apron, a doll with its clothes on and a piece of material for drying the doll. (See also Further activities 7, page 66.)

1 Let the children sit in a small group around the water tray and give each one a doll and an apron. Ask them to undress the dolls ready to give them a bath. When they have done this, ask them to tell you the order in which they took off the clothes. Could they choose which order to follow or did some garments have to be removed before others, e.g. coats before frocks?

2 Ask them to tell you how the dolls are different. They may mention size, weight, material from which they are made, eye colour, hair colour and other features. Can the dolls move their arms, legs, heads and eyes? What can Jenny do that the dolls cannot do? What does Jenny need that the dolls do not need? (Jenny is the baby in the picture in *Starter Book A*.)

3 Put the jugs of water out of reach of the children and ask if they can tell by looking which is the hot water. (Make sure that the hot water is hot enough to be steaming.) You can tell them that we call this cloud 'steam'.

4 Pour the cold water into the water tray first. Let the children feel it and describe what it feels like. Point out its various properties – it can be splashed, poured, sloshed about, it keeps its surface shiny and smooth if nobody is splashing, and so on. Use the word 'liquid' to describe it and encourage the children to notice that the water is colourless and clear.

5 Give the children some soap and let them wash their dolls. Find out if they know the parts of the body by saying, 'Wash your doll's face.' 'Wash your doll's elbows.' Ask them to find their own ankles, wrists and so on.

6 You could round this off by playing 'Simon says', naming parts of the body.

Activity B2—Soap

Observing and sorting soap by colour and size; matching smells

You need:

a selection of toilet soap of different varieties, and different sizes within the same variety (the children can bring examples from home and you can make a display); partly used samples of the same sizes and varieties; liquid soap; a foil dish; a small bowl; facilities for washing hands; sorting circles.

1 Put the selection of soaps in the middle of the table, removing the wrappers from the new ones. Let the children examine them and feel their shapes. Are there any with circles or ovals? Which of them have rectangles and curves?

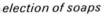
election of soaps

2 Sort them into broad colour sets and ask the children to name the shades of colour using 'deep' and 'pale'.

3 Place one large and one small tablet of soap of the same kind side by side and ask the children how they are the same and how they are different (size only).

4 If you have some liquid soap, squeeze a little into a foil dish. Ask the children how it looks and feels different from the other soaps. Take the opportunity to talk about what liquids do which solids do not do (at a very simple level).

5 Now look at the partly used soaps and ask the children what has happened to them. How are they different from the new pieces of soap? Help the children to notice the smaller size and the loss of shape. Why has this happened? What happens when we leave soap in the water? Get a small bowl of water, put a piece of soap in it and leave it for a few days. Let the children observe what happens. What happens when we use soap and get it wet? What happens when we leave the soap to dry off? Let the children set up investigations to answer these questions. Why do we have soap dishes?

6 Let the children choose whichever soap they like to wash their hands with. What does it feel like when hands are soapy? (Slippery, soft, smooth.) Why does Jenny's mother have to be very careful when she bathing Jenny?

7 Now choose six pieces of soap with very different smells and ask the children to smell each of them. Let each child in turn choose a soap without the rest of the group knowing which one, and let the child wash his or her hands and dry them. Can the other children tell which soap was used? How?

Activity B3—Teeth

Observing and investigating teeth and teeth cleaning

You need:

each child to bring from home his or her toothbrush and toothpaste in a labelled bag; each child will need a beaker and a margarine carton for teeth cleaning, and a biscuit to eat; a mirror so that the children can examine their teeth; small labels so that you can label their toothbrushes pieces of clean paper; sorting circles.

1 Ask the children to put their labelled toothbrushes on a clean piece of paper in the centre of the table. Are any of the toothbrushes exactly th same?

2 Sort the toothbrushes into colour sets and let the children decide where the various shades should go. Use 'deeper than' and 'paler than to describe them.

3 Ask the children if the toothbrushes are different in any other way. Some may have clear plastic handles, some may have a hole in the handle, some may be longer, shorter or more or less curved. Help the children to find the language to express the differences which they observe.

4 Ask the children to identify their toothbrushes by telling you two things about them. For example, 'Mine is the long blue one.' 'Mine is the green one which you can see through.'

5 Now let the children look at their teeth in the mirror. Give each of them a biscuit to eat and then let them look in the mirror again. How do their teeth look now? Much discussion may follow here about what is harmful to teeth.

6 Give each child a beaker, a margarine carton, his or her toothbrush an toothpaste, and show them how to clean their teeth correctly.

7 When they have cleaned their teeth, let them look in the mirror again and tell you how their teeth look different.

8 Ask them if they know how many teeth they have. Let them count each other's teeth and find out how many each has at the top and how many at the bottom. You could help them to record their results by constructing a simple block graph.

9 What are their front teeth like? What are their back teeth like? What are their front teeth used for? What are their back teeth used for? Which are the hardest to clean?

Activity B4—Mopping up

Investigating which materials will mop up water and which will not

You need:
equal-sized squares (30 cm side) of a variety of materials; a bowl; a tablespoon; water; two sorting circles.

1 Place all the pieces of material on the table and let the children look at them, feel them and describe them. Ask them how the pieces look different. Encourage them to describe colour differences and sort them into patterned and plain. Let the children feel the materials and describe how each piece feels. They may use words like 'soft', 'hairy', 'fluffy', 'smooth', 'thick', 'thin' and 'stretchy'. Encourage them to use words which are associated with properties which can only be discovered by feeling.

2 Ask the children now how the pieces of material are the same. They should be able to tell you that they are the same shape – square. They should also notice that they are the same size. Ask them how they can be sure that they are the same size. They may suggest comparing them by placing them one on top of the other.

3 Ask them now which they think would be good for mopping up water spilt in the bathroom. Let the children talk about this and make their suggestions. Ask them if they can think of a way of finding out. If they come up with a reasonable idea let them pursue it; otherwise, suggest that you put a measured amount of water in the bowl and find out which pieces of material can mop up all the water and which cannot. Let them do this and sort the squares accordingly. (Use about six tablespoons of water – or whatever is appropriate for your squares.)

...ich will mop up water?

4 You can continue this activity by asking the children which piece of material they think will dry first. Let them make their predictions, then hang the pieces up to dry and see if their predictions were right.

Activity B5—Toys

Sorting toys by various properties, including material and sink/float

You need:

the children should bring from home toys which they play with in the bath; labels for the toys; a variety of water toys – boats, fish, ducks, diver and wind-up toys; a water tray; waterproof aprons for the children; two sorting circles.

1 Put all the toys on the table and give the children time to handle them and talk about them. If you have several boats, for example, put these in one of the sorting circles and ask the children to tell you how they are different. Then point out that you have put them all in one sorting circle. Why have you done this? How are the things in the circle the same? Repeat this with any other toys of which you have a sufficient number.

2 Put the toys together again and this time select one toy which is hard and one which is soft. Let the children feel the toys and talk about 'hard' and 'soft'. Then put the hard toy in one circle and the soft toy in the other circle and ask the children to sort the rest of the toys according to whether they are hard or soft.
3 Talk about the toys and ask the children if they can sort the toys according to the material from which they are made. They will produc a number of sets. Can they now explore the classroom and find things made of the same materials and put these in their appropriate sets wit the toys? In doing this, encourage the children to talk about their reasons for considering that the objects are made of the same materia Encourage them to make observations using the appropriate senses, and to make observations which are appropriate for the task.
4 Collect the toys together again and let the children use the water tray find out which toys sink and which toys float. Let them put the toys into the sorting circles according to whether they sink or float. The children can draw a picture to record their results.

Activity B6—Steamed up

Investigating steaming up; predicting what will steam up

You need:

a mirror tile; a ceramic tile; a square or rectangular piece of glass with its edges protected; a jug of cold water; a jug of steaming water; some pap tissues; a collection of objects for the children to predict whether or not they will steam up – include both shiny and dull objects that do steam u as well as (if possible) shiny ones that do not.

1 Begin by letting the children handle the mirror, the tile and the piece of glass. Encourage the children to look at them, feel them and talk about their observations. Ask them how the objects are different and how they are the same, e.g. flat, hard, shiny, cold. What shape are they?

2 Tell the children that you are going to pretend that the tile and the mirror are on the bathroom wall and that the piece of glass is part of the window. Hold the tile, the mirror and the piece of glass over the bowl of hot water and explain that this is a pretend bath of hot water. Ask the children to describe what happens. When the objects are sufficiently steamed up, let the children touch them and describe what it feels like. If you place a tissue on the wet surfaces, the children will be able to see that the moisture is soaked up.

3 Bring out your collection of objects and let the children try to predict (with reasons) which ones will get steamed up. The reasons may be quite wrong but the main purpose is to encourage the children to think and start making predictions (or sensible suggestions). (On page 101, you will find a note about prediction in science.)

Making and doing activities

The problem for the child is:

'Can you make a boat from a matchbox tray which you can play with in the bath? Can you make it so that it will carry a cargo of six 1p pieces?'

You need:

a large bowl of water (or the water tray); some 1p pieces; cellophane; foil; small polythene bags; waterproof adhesive; a matchbox tray for each child.

Encourage the children to approach this problem along these lines.

1 The problem — Can you make a boat from a matchbox tray which you can play with in the bath? Can you make it carry a cargo of six 1p pieces?

2 Exploring the problem — What does the boat need to do? Will it be treated roughly or gently? Will it always stay on top of the water? Is a matchbox tray likely to make a good boat? Is it made of a suitable material? What are the properties of that material? Will it stay afloat? Is it waterproof?

3 Ideas for solving the problem — The matchbox will need to be made waterproof. What materials do we have that are waterproof? Do you know, or shall we have to find out? How can we make it stay afloat if it doesn't do it by itself? What have we got that will help it float?

4 Making

The children will have to decide how to use the materials to wrap the matchbox to make it waterproof, and in such a way that the wrapping does not become water-logged. Make sure that the glue used is waterproof. There will, no doubt be a great deal of testing before they are satisfied with their efforts.

5 Evaluating

Does it float? Does it stay afloat? Does it get soggy? Does it carry its cargo?

Further activities

Some suggestions

1 Ask the children to bring new bars of soap into school, so that you can make a display of different kinds of soap. Make a block graph to show the relative popularity of different kinds of soap

2 Ask the school nurse to come and talk to your class about teeth. Follow this by collecting pictures from magazines of foods which are bad for your teeth and those which are good.

3 Ask a child to lie down on the floor on a piece of paper and let the others draw round him or her. They can draw in his or her eyes, ears, etc. Help the children to make labels and label their drawing. Then let them do the same individually, using the outline of a doll. Help them make the labels for the body parts and stick these on their own outlines. They can use the big drawing for matching.

4 Give each child a piece of plasticine and some beads. Can they make model of their bottom teeth and get the right number of beads representing their teeth?

5 Look at plastic and metal tubes, e.g. bubble bath, toothpaste. What happens when the children squeeze the tube? What happens when they let go? When it is empty can they fill it again? How was it filled originally?

6 Sort classroom objects for float/sink. Can the children find something big to float? Can they find something heavy to float? etc.

7 Ask a mother to come in and bath her baby in the classroom. Ask her talk about looking after a baby.

The cook

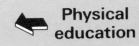 Physical education

 Language

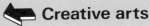 Creative arts

 Mathematics

Science

Science activities

Further activities

Introduction

Science activities

The kitchen setting provides a variety of familiar starting points for children. In previous topics, the children have been introduced to the cone and the cylinder, and the activities here enable them to investigate the properties of these shapes further. They have looked at shapes whic roll and the rolling pin provides another example.

The variety of foodstuffs in the kitchen provides an opportunity for observation. The children use their observations to identify differences and similarities, and then to distinguish one foodstuff from another. Gre care should be taken to emphasise that nothing must ever be tasted if w do not know that it is a foodstuff.

Another important objective of this topic is the extension of children': experiences with solids and liquids. Pouring and the fact that a liquid ha no shape of its own are explored. The children are encouraged to observ the similarity in the pouring properties of substances such as dry sand ai sugar as well as water and cooking oil.

Making and doing activities

Two problems for the children are suggested:
- i 'Can you separate rice from salt?'
- ii 'Can you make something from a sheet of paper that will help to p salt from a jar into a salt pot?'

It is anticipated that the children will attempt to solve the first problem b making some sort of a sieve but other suggestions may emerge which ca be investigated. The second problem is likely to produce attempts to make a simple funnel.

The cook   Science activities

Activity Co1 — Sugar

Observing differences and similarities between different types of sugar

You need:

granulated sugar; caster sugar; demerara sugar; three plates; a sieve which will let the granulated and caster sugars through but not the demerara sugar; magnifying glasses; a piece of kitchen paper for each child.

Warning

This activity involves tasting.
You must emphasise to the children that we only taste things that we know are food. We never taste anything else. They must not taste anything in the classroom unless you tell them to do so. Make sure that the activity is carried out under hygienic conditions – wash hands, use a table cloth, etc.

1 Put small amounts of each type of sugar on separate plates and pass these round for the children to see. If possible, let them use a magnifying glass to help their observation.
2 Ask how they are different. The children will probably see the difference in colour immediately but ask them to look again closely fc another difference.
3 Suggest that they take a pinch of sugar from each plate and rub it between finger and thumb. Let them put their pinches of sugar on to their pieces of kitchen paper. For each type of sugar, ask them to describe how it feels.

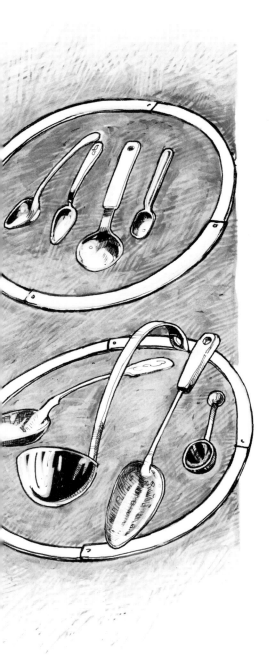

4 Suggest now that they taste a little of each type of sugar and describe how it tastes. Can they detect how the taste is the same and how it is different?

5 Let them taste the sugars again and this time ask how each type feels on their tongues.

6 Now show the children a sieve and ask them to tell you about it and where they have seen one before. What is it for? How does it work?

7 Ask them what they think will happen to each type of sugar when it is put in the sieve. Try this and ask the children to describe what happens in each case.

8 Can they tell you why the brown sugar will not go through the sieve?

Activity Co2—Spoons

Sorting spoons using various criteria; estimating the relative capacity of spoons

You need:
a wide variety of spoons of different sizes and materials, and for different purposes; dry fine sand; water; sorting circles.

1 Put together all the spoons which could be used for eating, including metal and plastic spoons. Ask the children why they think you have put all these spoons in the same set.

2 Now draw their attention to the set of spoons which we do not use for eating and see if they can tell you why each would be unsuitable. They might say, 'It's too big', 'It's too heavy', or 'Its handle is too long'.

3 If you feel the children are able, you may wish to sort the spoons according to other attributes – material, length, shape of handle or purpose.

4 Now put all the spoons together and ask the children to guess which would hold the most.

5 Let the children play with the spoons using sand and water. See if they can agree which one holds the most. (Observing their method of measuring will give you an indication of their level of thinking.)

Activity Co3—Fats

Observing and investigating the nature of solid and liquid fats – margarine, lard and cooking oil

You need:
margarine; lard; cooking oil; teaspoons; a plastic knife for each child; three saucers; a kitchen roll.

Warning

This activity involves tasting.
Tell the children that they are going to taste the fats. We know that the fats are food we eat and you, the teacher, have told them it is safe to taste them. They must never taste anything which is not a foodstuff they usually eat. In the classroom, they must never taste anything unless they are told to by the teacher.

Note
Children whose culture regards the pig as unclean should not be asked or allowed to taste lard. Children of this age may be unaware of this fact but their parents might be greatly offended if the children are subjected to this experience.

1 Tell the children they will be handling food and remind them to wash their hands.

2 Take a level teaspoonful of margarine and put this on to a saucer so that the margarine retains the shape of the spoon.

3 Now give the children a plastic knife each and let them take a tiny amount of margarine. Suggest that they taste it and describe what it tastes like. How does it feel in their mouths? What do their lips feel like?

4 Let half the group rub a tiny amount of margarine on to the back of one of their hands. Ask them to describe how it feels. Does it make their hands look different?

5 Repeat these steps (2–4) with the lard but let the other half of the group put the lard on their hands.

6 Ask the children how the margarine and lard look different on the saucers. Do they look the same in any way? Did they taste different or the same? Did they feel different or the same? Did the children's lips feel different or the same?

7 Now take a spoonful of oil and put this on a saucer. What shape is the oil now? What shape was it in the spoon? How is it different from the margarine and the lard? (The margarine and lard retain the shape of the spoon; the oil spreads out as far as it can.)

8 Let them taste the oil and then rub a little on the back of their other hands. Ask them if their two hands look different or feel different. How are margarine, lard and cooking oil the same?

9 Tell the children to go to the tap and let some cold water run over the backs of their hands before they use soap to wash them. What happens when water touches the backs of their hands? How are margarine, lard and cooking oil the same?

10 Put a little of each fat on to a piece of kitchen roll. What happens?

Activity Co4—Sugar and salt

Observing differences and similarities between sugar and salt

You need:
a bag of flour; a bowl; a sieve; water; four yoghurt cartons; kitchen paper; a salt pot containing a little table salt; a sugar bowl containing a little granulated sugar; a shopping bag containing an unlabelled jar of granulated sugar, an unlabelled jar of table salt and two labels: 'sugar' and 'salt'; a magnifying glass.

1 Tell the children to wash their hands.

2 Tell the children you are going to make some play dough. Measure a yoghurt cartonful of flour and ask the children to tell you when they think that it is level. Measure out three more cartonfuls.

3 Now let one of the children tip the flour into the bowl, counting the cartons as they are emptied. Ask the children to notice how the flour falls and to describe it. Does it fall all at once or a little at a time? Give the children an opportunity to look at flour through a magnifying glass and let them tell you what they see.

4 Tell them that the other thing they will need will be salt and produce your shopping bag. Take out the jars and 'discover' that the labels have fallen off. Point out that since this is all that was in your shopping bag, one jar must be sugar and one jar must be salt.

5 Tell the children that they will have to help you decide which is which.

6 Put a small sample from each of the jars on a piece of paper and ask the children what is the same about them. They will be able to tell you that they are the same colour.

7 Suggest that they rub each one between their fingers and thumbs and ask again if they feel the same or different.

8 Suggest that they look at them through a magnifying glass and tell you whether they look the same or different.

9 Ask the children if they think they will both go through the sieve and let them try.

10 Is there any difference in smell?

11 Suggest that it might be possible to compare them with some more sugar and salt. Look around and 'discover' your salt pot and sugar bowl. Let the children examine the contents of these in the same way (steps 6–10).

12 Can they now tell you which is the sugar jar and which is the salt jar?

13 Having decided which is salt, let a child fill two yoghurt cartons with salt and tip them into the bowl with the flour. Ask the children to notice how the salt falls. Does it fall like flour or like sugar?

14 Now add enough water to make the dough and let the children play with it.

Activity Co5—Rolling pins

Observing and investigating the properties of a rolling pin: the shape (cylinder) and material (wood)

You need:
play dough, play pastry or plasticine; a wooden rolling pin; an empty washing-up container; any other roughly cylindrical objects which might be used as substitute rolling pins, e.g. a piece of plastic drainpipe, a piece of broomstick, the cardboard middle of a kitchen roll.

1 Let the children play with the dough or plasticine and when they are ready suggest that they make some biscuits for you. Let them flatten the material by hand at this stage.

2 Now ask them how the cook will flatten the pastry. When they have made their suggestions, show them a wooden rolling pin. Pass it round for the children to look at and feel. Ask them to tell you about it. What does the wood look like? Can they see the grain of the wood?

3 What can they tell you about how it feels? Suggest that they rub their fingers along the rolling pin; they should notice that it is smooth. They may also tell you that it is curved. Encourage them to press it and tell you that it is hard.

4 Ask them now how it moves. Find out if they know its shape. Do they know what shape is at each end? Are the two ends the same? Do they know what it is made of? If they do not tell them that it is a cylinder with circles at the ends, and it is made of wood.

5 Now let the children pretend that they have not got a rolling pin. What could they use instead? Remind them that it must work like a rolling pin. What shape must it be? What must it feel like?

6 Let the children use things which they can find in the classroom for rolling their pastry and encourage each child to tell the others about his or her problems: 'Mine won't roll' or 'Mine's too rough.'

7 Are the things they are using made of wood? Does the material they a made of look like the wood of the rolling pin? Does it feel like it? Is it hard?

8 'Discover' an empty washing-up container. Ask the children if they think it will be suitable for rolling pastry. Let them try it. Does it work well?

9 Can they tell you why it does not work or what they could do to make work better?

Activity Co6—Funnels

Investigating the properties of a cone; investigating pouring

You need:
a cone-shaped funnel; a large jug; a large narrow-necked bottle into which the funnel will fit; a bowl of fine dry sand.

1 Put on the table the bowl of sand and the narrow-necked bottle. (Kee the jug and funnel out of sight.) Ask one of the children to pour the sand into the bottle without spilling any.

2 Stop the child when difficulty is encountered and ask what might be done to make the task easier. Children may suggest shaping their hands to make a small hole to let the sand through or they may sugges a jug for pouring. Let the children try these suggestions and talk abou what happens.

3 Ask them if they can think of anything else which might work. When their discussion focuses on the idea of a funnel, produce yours and make sure they know what it is called. Ask them what shape it is. What does it remind them of? Can they remember the word 'cone'?

4 Direct their attention to the shape at each end of the funnel. How is the top different from the bottom? Encourage them to say that one circle is bigger or smaller than the other.

5 Now ask one child to place the funnel inside the neck of the bottle and another to pour the sand from the bowl into the funnel.

6 Encourage them to describe what is happening, using words like 'pouring', 'flowing', 'wide' and 'narrow'.

Activity Co7—Currants and spice

Selecting appropriate ways to distinguish between flour, sugar, currants and spice

You need:
flour; sugar; currants; mixed spice; four yoghurt cartons containing samples of these hidden by a paper tissue, held in place with a rubber band; a bun tin; a magnifying glass.

1 Remind the children that they will be handling food so they need to wash their hands.

2 Put a small amount of flour, sugar, currants and spice separately into the compartments of a bun tin.

3 Let the children now try to identify the contents of the bun tin. Watch them to see which senses they use. Make sure that each child has smelled the contents and felt them.

4 Now produce the yoghurt cartons containing the samples and ask the children to think how they could find out which of the substances is in each of the cartons without looking or feeling.

5 Pass the cartons round and see what the children do. Leave the bun tin on the table to remind the children what they are trying to identify.

6 If they try to smell them suggest that they look again at the bun tin and tell you which one has a smell. (If the tissue hides the smell too much, you could make a few pin holes in it.)

7 They should be able to pick out the spice by smelling. Put this on one side.

8 Now ask if they can find another way of telling what is in the other cartons. Let them talk about this; eventually, they will probably pick up the cartons and shake them. Tell them to do this close to their ear and listen for the quietest sound and the loudest sound.

9 Now suggest that they look at the flour, the sugar and the fruit in the bun tin and guess which would make the quietest and the loudest noises if they were in cartons. Which things do the children now think are in the cartons?

10 Let the children look in the cartons to see if their guesses were right. Can they tell you why they thought the flour would be the quietest?

Activity Co8—Liquid

Investigating the nature of a liquid (water) and a solid (plasticine)

You need:

a few flat plastic plates; plastic bowls; plastic knives, forks and spoons; two saucepans; water; plasticine; playhouse facilities.

1 When the children are ready to start making the pretend dinner, tell them that you would like to start with soup. Make sure that they have access to water and a saucepan to use on the pretend cooker in the playhouse.

2 When they tell you that the soup is ready, ask them to pour some for each of you. Ask them, before they do the pouring, which it is better to use – plates or bowls.

3 Suggest that two of you in the group have bowls and two of you plates, and see how you get on eating your soup. You will of course have spoons.

4 Ask the children whether the bowl or plate is better for soup. How is one better than the other? Encourage words such as 'deeper' and 'curved'. Ask them why this matters . Talk to them about how the soup spreads out as the cooking oil did. It does not have a shape of its own. It takes up the shape of the container. Use the word 'liquid' but accompany the word with descriptive comments like 'can be poured', 'splashes', 'spills', etc. Reinforce understanding in this way until you are quite sure that the word 'liquid' conveys all these ideas to the children.

5 Ask them now what you are going to have next. (If they have a whole pretend dinner, suggest that they now use plasticine but remind them not to eat it.)

plasticine
fish and chips

'soup'

6 Let a child serve the pretend dinner on plates and ask the children which it is better to use – spoons or knives and forks. Point out that the plasticine stays in a lump and does not take the shape of its container, and while you are talking to them link these ideas with the word 'solid'.

7 Pretend that each of you has a large (plasticine) piece of meat or fish which is obviously too big for the mouth.

8 Suggest that two of you try with spoons and two of you with knives and forks. Discuss with the children what happens. Ask them why we need a knife to help us eat sometimes. Do we need a knife to eat soup? Do we need a knife to eat liquids? What do we need a knife for?

9 Afterwards, the children might like to draw pictures of things we drink out of cups and glasses – liquids. They might also like to try to draw pictures of things which we have to bite with our teeth or cut with a knife – solids.

Making and doing activities

i The problem for the child is:
   'Can you separate rice from salt?'

You need:
a mixture of rice and salt; rice; salt; various kinds of scrap materials which might be useful in making rudimentary sieves; plastic containers; various kinds of paper; sellotape; rubber bands.

1 The problem	Can you separate rice from salt?
2 Exploring the problem	How are rice and salt different? Can you use any of these differences to separate them?
3 Ideas for solving the problem	Let the children make their suggestions. These may include picking the rice out by hand, washing the rice with water to dissolve the salt, making a sieve with holes big enough to let the salt through but not the rice. Remind the children what happened when you sieved different types of sugar.
	There may be other ideas. Let the children talk through their ideas and decide what they would like to try.
4 Making	Let them pursue their ideas and discuss how well they work. If any of them do want to wash the salt off, make sure that they use a small amount of water. Discuss the problem of getting the salt back out of the water and when this remains unresolved, arrange to leave the water with the salt in a warm place. Eventually, the water will evaporate and you will be able to see the salt crystals left behind. (A magnifying glass is useful.)
	Those who attempt to make sieves will be greatly helped by a careful choice of materials.
5 Evaluating	The children will be able to see that an efficient sieve is the quickest way of separating the rice and salt. You might be able to show them a garden sieve or borrow a set of graded sieves from the science department of your local secondary school.

ii The problem for the child is:
   'Can you make something from a sheet of paper which will help you put salt from a jar into a salt pot?'

You need:
a large jar of salt; a small salt pot; a variety of sheets of paper; paper clips; sellotape.

e and
t

ce
net
rtain
eve)

SALT

RICE

This is a well known problem and you can let the children tackle it along the usual lines.

1 The problem	Can you make something from a sheet of paper which will help you to put salt from a jar into a salt pot?
2 Exploring the problem	What is salt like? What does it do? What is the salt pot like? How big is its hole? Let the children do this over a large sheet of paper to catch spills. Show the children how to scoop up the paper and direct the salt back into the large jar.
3 Ideas for solving the problem	The children will remember that they used a funnel in an earlier activity; they may realise that they could make a paper one. They may have other simpler ideas, such as making a chute.
4 Making	The children will probably need to help each other to manipulate paper and sellotape. Encourage them to do this.
5 Evaluating	You can have a competition to see whose funnel works best. Who can pour the salt in with the least amount spilt?

Further activities

Some suggestions

1 Find out more about what cooks in big kitchens do. Let the school cook come and talk about the job.
2 Ask the children to find out from home the things they eat which have sugar in them. Suggest that they cut out pictures from magazines to make a wall display.
3 Visit a real baker's shop so that the children can see the variety of shapes into which bread is made. They could then use play dough to make their own baker's shop.
4 Compare kitchen utensils, e.g. two bowls, two pans, to see which holds more and which holds less. Do this by pouring directly from one to the other.
5 Make cakes, biscuits, rice dishes, etc. and let the children observe and investigate ingredients and utensils.
6 Listen to sounds made by tapping with implements made from wood, metal, plastic, etc.
7 Practise dance movements related to cooking activities, e.g. stirring, rolling out, washing up, boiling and bubbling, dough stretching, and being rolled out.

The caretaker

Language ➡

Mathematics ➡

⬅ **Physical education**

⬅ **Creative arts**

⬇

Science

⬅ ⬇ ➡

People and their jobs and occupations
Starter Book page 26

Science activities

Ca1 Nails and screws   78
Observing differences and similarities between nails and screws; sorting nails and screws

Ca2 Polishing   79
Observing and investigating some properties of metal and wood

Ca3 Marks   80
Investigating how to remove marks

Ca4 Scissors   81
Investigating what scissors will cut and what they will not cut

Making and doing
Teachers' Book page 82

⬇

Further activities
Teachers' Book page 83

Introduction

Science activities

In this topic, there is continuing emphasis on the most basic of scientific activities, observing. Children are asked to observe, using whichever senses will give the most useful and appropriate information. Other activities, such as sorting, are introduced now almost as a matter of routine.

You should also be beginning to think in this way and should be encouraging the children to develop their skills in working inquisitively, observantly and with some system. This is not something which will happen overnight: the aim is gradually to establish not only a developing range of skills but also an attitude which will cause those skills to be used.

You will notice in this topic that reference is made to the development of some ideas about materials (wood and metal) and energy. We are moving little by little towards understanding. A lot of evidence and experience needs to be accumulated before children fully understand these ideas, and they need continuous help. You will find further discussion about the development of understanding of concepts on pages 110 and 127.

Making and doing activities

Two problems for the children are suggested:
  i 'Can you make a model of a screw?'
  ii 'Can you make something from wood?'
The first of these activities allows the children to explore the thread of screws. The other provides them with an opportunity to use their imaginations and a few nails! It is particularly important to ensure that the girls are involved and are not back seat passengers. Do not let the boys do all the constructive work. Make sure that the girls also learn how to use a hammer and any other tools which you feel you can provide.

It is of course essential that the children should be shown how to hold tools correctly and how to use them safely. It must be emphasised that they should be conscious of the need not only to look after themselves but also to be aware of the safety of others.

The caretaker   Science activities

Activity Ca1 — Nails and screws

Observing differences and similarities between nails and screws; sorting nails and screws

You need:
a box of nails of three distinctly different lengths and head sizes; a similar box of screws including brass as well as steel ones; three hammers of different sizes appropriate to the nail sizes; three screwdrivers to fit the screws provided; a few blocks of soft wood; a sorting tray.

1 Give the children a variety of nails and screws. Choose one large nail and one large screw and ask the children what is different about them. Show them the thread on the screw and the groove on its head. Can they describe the similarities? (The nails and screws all have a point at one end and a head at the other end. They are all hard and shiny. The nails and some of the screws are the same colour.) Talk about the material from which the nails and screws are made. Help the children to sort out their ideas about what metals are like. (Metals are strong, hard, shiny, make a noise when dropped or struck, can be finely worked, etc.) Ask the children to put the screws back in the box and to leave the nails on the table.

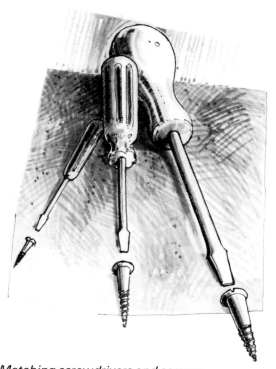

Matching screwdrivers and screws

2 Examine the nails with the children. How are they different? Draw their attention to length and head size. Ask the children to sort the nails for length. Put one of each length in the compartments of the sorting tray as a guide for them to match.

3 Put the nails back in the box and bring out the screws. Ask again for differences. This time, pay particular attention to head size. Ask the children to sort the screws according to head size and again put one of each in the sorting tray as a guide.

4 Leave the screws in the sorting tray and produce the hammers and screwdrivers. Ask what they are and what they are used for. Can the children mime the action to show how each is used? Look again at the screws in the sorting tray and ask the children to match the screwdrivers to the screws they fit. Now ask the children to choose a nail from the box to match each hammer.

5 Provide the children with some soft wood blocks and show them how to hammer a nail in safely. They will enjoy doing this. Discuss with them the idea that they are having to use a lot of hard hits to make the nail go in. (They are being alerted to the idea that to do the job they are having to use energy – although it is too soon to put it in those terms to the children.)

6 You could take the children round the school and show them where nails and screws have been used. Why is a nail used in one place and a screw in another? The children could look for their own examples and try to explain why they are there.

Activity Ca2—Polishing

Observing and investigating some properties of metal and wood

You need:

a collection of shiny and dull objects, including polished and unpolished wood, shiny and dull metal (some of the metal should be shiny because of its nature, e.g. chromium, some should be polished, e.g. brass or copper), sheets of dull paper, sheets of shiny paper; each child will need a rag with some metal polish on it, a metal teaspoon, some solid furniture polish and a duster.

1 Give the children the shiny and dull pieces of wood. Let them tell you everything they can about the pieces of wood – try to encourage discussion of what wood is like. Let them talk about its appearance, how hard it is, what sort of noise it makes when it is dropped (contrast metals). They will notice how the grain shows up more noticeably in the polished piece. Can they tell you how we can make wood shine?

2 Present the children with a collection of other objects and ask them to look for the shiny and dull ones. As the children discuss the objects, ask them which could be polished. Start a display table for dull things and a table for shiny things. The children may bring things from home to add to these.

3 Take your group around the school to look for dull surfaces and shiny surfaces. Your caretaker may be willing to talk to the children about which surfaces he or she has to polish and show them how it is done and what is used.

4 Give each child a rag with a little metal polish on it and a metal spoon. Let the children polish their spoons. Help them to observe carefully what happens. What happens to the spoon? What colour comes off on the rag? (As in the case of the wooden blocks, take the opportunity here to encourage discussion of the properties of metals – appearance, hardness, sound when dropped, etc.)

5 Now let the children polish a wooden surface, e.g. a cupboard door, chair or desk, using solid furniture polish. Help them to make observations as before and to notice differences between polishing metal and wood.

6 Remind them to wash their hands as they have been using cleaning materials.

Activity Ca3—Marks

Investigating how to remove marks

You need:

a plastic topped table (Formica or similar); a small piece of plastic coated board; some chalk; some milk; a wax crayon; poster paint; a pencil; PVA adhesive; dry dusters; a bowl of water; some scouring powder and rough cloths.

(The activity is set in a classroom which has plastic-topped tables.)

1 Ask the children why their classroom tables need cleaning every afternoon when they go home. What sort of things get on the tables to make them dirty? They may suggest several of the following – chalk, paint, plasticine, pencil, wax crayon, felt-tip pen, adhesive, milk. Choose about five of the children's suggestions and ask if they know which are easy to get off the tables and which are hard to get off. Suggest the children try to find out.

2 Use one table and let the children mark patches with the five materials e.g. chalk, milk (let it dry), wax crayon, paint, pencil. (On the small piece of board, provide an example of a material which will not come off even when scrubbed with scouring powder – PVA adhesive.) Do the children think that any of the marks will come off with a dry duster? Let one of them try. Did any come off easily? Did any come off with hard rubbing? Which ones did not come off?

paint

milk

pencil

wax crayon

duster

chalk

3 Now try the same routine with a damp cloth and finally with a damp cloth and scouring powder.
4 Use this scheme for a table display of their results. Put the actual samples on the table as well as their names. The children may notice that the display shows how the methods of cleaning are increasingly effective but do not stress this point if they do not notice.

DRY CLOTH		DAMP CLOTH WATER		DAMP CLOTH WATER SCOURING POWDER	
yes	**no**	**yes**	**no**	**yes**	**no**
chalk	milk wax crayon paint pencil P.V.A.	chalk milk paint	wax crayon pencil P.V.A.	chalk milk paint wax crayon pencil	P.V.A.

5 Talk to the children about how they can help the caretaker and the cleaners. Which things should they try very hard not to get on the tables?

Activity Ca4—Scissors

Investigating what scissors will cut and what they will not cut

You need:
a few dinner knives of different shapes; a pair of school scissors for each child; sheets of thin paper, some oddments of thicker paper and card, pieces of different fabrics (all for cutting up).

1 Ask the children what they use to cut their food. Look at the dinner knives. Which part cuts the food? Ask the children which part of the knife they should hold. Why should they not put food into their mouths with the knives? What do they have to do to cut their food? (Push the knife hard on the food; this is hard work, using energy.)
2 What is used to cut paper? Look at a pair of school scissors. Which parts cut the paper? How should scissors be held – when cutting, walking across the room with them, and passing them to somebody?
3 What are knives and scissors made of? Are they dull or shiny? Are they hard or soft?
4 How good are school scissors? Give each child a pair of scissors and some paper and fabric to cut. Suggest that they sort the materials according to whether the scissors will or will not cut them.
5 Some of the children may like to find out how many sheets of thin paper their scissors can cut at once. Do they all find the same answer? Does the answer depend on who does the cutting or on which scissors they use?

Making and doing activities

i The problem for the child is:
   'Can you make a model of a screw?'

You need:
plasticine; a nail or similar to scrape the plasticine.

1	The problem	Can you make a model of a screw?
2	Exploring the problem	This is confined to carefully examining screws discover the path of the screw groove. The children will find it easier with a really big screw or you may be able to provide some big plastic screws from a children's model making set.
3	Ideas for solving the problem	If the children have grasped the idea that the groove goes up the screw in a spiral, they may either consider scratching a groove on a plasticine cylinder or cone or using a plasticine worm to act as the thread.
4	Making	The children's success will depend firstly on whether they have been able to pick out the ide of the spiral thread and, secondly, on their manual dexterity.
5	Evaluating	How many of the children do manage to produ a spiral? (This is not an easy concept to grasp.) Let those who have managed talk about the ide Have they seen a circular ramp in a car park? Why are these used?

ii The problem for the child is:
   'Can you make something from wood?'

You need:
an assortment of pieces of soft wood; nails and hammers.

This is not a problem in the same sense as the other problems which hav been suggested. The objective can be interpreted much more widely. What the children decide to make will be determined largely by the piec of wood which you are able to provide. Do not confine your supplies to very small pieces if you can avoid it. Some children think big!

Further activities

Some suggestions

1 Get the school caretaker to come and talk about his or her job. What do caretakers do during the school holidays?
2 Look at nuts and bolts. Examine the threads on the bolts. Match nuts to bolts by size. Which way do you turn the nut to screw it on and off? Is it always the same?
3 Draw spirals on pieces of paper and let the children cut them out. Hang them by the centre so that they turn in the draught.

hang from this point

Discuss the fact that the paper is all in one piece.

4 Make a collection of things that are so shiny you can see your face in them. What do you look like in a flat surface? What do you look like in a curved surface, e.g. the front or the back of a spoon?
5 Mime the actions of sawing, hammering, polishing, sweeping, etc.
6 Make a collection of brushes of various shapes and sizes. Which ones does the caretaker find most useful? What are they for? Why are they that size or shape?
7 Make a collection of keys. The children can sort them in various ways.
8 Discuss litter with the children. What do we throw away? Why? Where do we put it? Why?

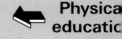

Language

Mathematics

Physica education

Creative arts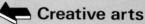

Science

People and their jobs and occupations

Starter Book page 28

Science activities

Making and doing

Teachers' Book page 94

Further activities
Teachers' Book page 95

Introduction

Science activities

In this topic, various settings have been included to reflect different children's experience and expectations.

Two concepts are given particular attention: freezing and melting, and evaporation. Freezing and melting have been considered before and the ideas are further developed here. Attention is focused on evaporation and there is some exploration of what that word embraces. There is no need to introduce the word itself at this stage unless it is clear it would be useful for the child. It is all too easy, once the child can use the general term, wrongly to assume that he or she understands the various ideas it covers. With words like 'evaporation', there can be many different levels of understanding. It is useful to find out what the children mean if they use such words. Their meaning can well be very narrow and limited, and there is the danger of reading into their use of such words more understanding than actually exists. Every opportunity to explore with the children phenomena such as freezing, melting and evaporation must be taken.

Making and doing activities

The problem for the child is:
  'Can you make a model tent?'
This problem offers plenty of scope for the imagination and for linked activities of various kinds.

School holidays   Science activities

Activity Sc1 — Sand and water

Observing and investigating differences and similarities between dry sand and water

You need:
a variety of equipment suitable for dry sand and a separate set for water (include jugs, cups, spoons, funnels, sieves, watering cans, squeezy bottles); a selection of opaque jars or bottles with stoppers or screw caps; a sand tray containing dry sand; a bowl of water; some paper tissues; a magnifying glass; teaspoons; a metal tray on each table; salt; flour; icing sugar; granulated sugar; cooking oil; coloured water; paint water; vinegar; two clear plastic bottles (matched) with screw caps; each child will need two margarine cartons and a stone.

1 Gather the children around the bowl of water and remind them about the things which they have done with water when they have been playing round the water tray. Show them how water can be poured from a jug into a cup, and how it can be poured from a watering can. Then use a funnel to fill a squeezy bottle and let the water trickle through your fingers.
2 Now let the children go to the sand tray and ask them to do the same actions with the dry sand. Did they succeed? Encourage them to talk about the differences and similarities between sand and water.
3 Now show them how with a squeezy bottle you can make water go up, down, across and anywhere else you want to send it. Can they do this with dry sand? Let them try (with careful supervision). Why is it so much more difficult with sand than with water?
4 Let the children take some cartons of dry sand and some water to their tables. Ask them how the sand and water look different. They may tell you that the water is shiny and the sand is not and that they can see through the water but not through the sand. Ask them what colour

the sand is. Does water have a colour? Give them a magnifying glass to examine the water and the sand. Can they describe the difference? Can they see that sand is really a lot of separate little bits whereas the water is all joined together?

5   Let them try to get as much water as possible on to a teaspoon and then as much sand as possible on to another teaspoon. How do they look different? Encourage the children to use the words 'level' and 'heaped', 'more than' and 'less than'.

6   Give them each a stone and tell them to put their stones in their cartons of sand. When they do this, the stone rests on the top. They must push it down if they want it to go to the bottom. Now let them put water into their other cartons, and put the stone into the water. What happens this time?

7   Suggest that they feel the water with one hand and the sand with the other. How do they feel different? How do their hands look different afterwards?

8   Give the children various opaque containers and suggest that each of them puts either sand or water into their containers without the other seeing. Can the other children find out what is in the containers by shaking them?

9   Part fill one clear plastic bottle with sand and one with water. Pass the two bottles round and let the children shake them. How do they sound different? How do they look different? What can you see in the water? Are there any bubbles in the sand? Now fill each bottle completely and shake them again. How are they different? Why is there no sound?

10 Suggest that they empty their cartons of sand back into the sand tray by pouring the sand down a metal tray sloping into the sand tray. Ask them to describe what happens when the sand hits the metal tray. What does it sound like? Now let them do the same with water into the bowl. Draw their attention to the splashing and ask them how the water looks and sounds different from the sand.

11 Give them two pieces of tissue and ask them to clean out their cartons. What does the tissue look like in each case? Can they tell you what has happened? Can they tell you anything else which they think would soak into a tissue?

12 Give them some tissues and a variety of things to try. You can include salt, flour, icing sugar, granulated sugar, cooking oil, coloured water, paint water and vinegar. They may notice a number of things. With the paint water, they may notice that the water runs through the tissue beyond the paint. Do they have any ideas why this happens?

Activity Sc2—Wet sand

Investigating the differences in behaviour between wet sand and dry sand

You need:

two bowls of dry sand; a jug of water; a cup; a funnel; a sieve; a plate; two margarine cartons; a set of balance scales; a 20 cm circle of paper for each child; a supply of paper clips.

1 Have two bowls of dry sand on the table. Let the children take handfuls of the sand and let it trickle through their fingers. Suggest that they take a cupful from one bowl and pour it into the other. Can they describe how the sand moves? Try to establish that it pours but it is not continuous like water: it is made up of lots of little bits.

2 Take a margarine carton and fill one third of it with water. Fill another carton with dry sand and make sure that the children are aware that it is full. Now gradually empty the carton of dry sand into the water in the other carton so that you have a carton of wet sand and all the dry sand has been added. Talk to the children about what you are doing. Fill the dry sand carton again and put it on one of the balance pans. Now ask the children what they think will happen when you put the carton of wet sand on the other pan. Will the pans balance or will one side go down and the other up? Which pan will go down? What does this mean? Let the children talk about this and then put the wet sand carton on the balance pan and see what happens. Talk to them about the result and discuss what it means. (They will need much experience of using the balance to establish confidence in the results they observe.)

3 Ask the children if they have ever been on a beach on a windy day. What happens to the dry sand? You can put a small amount of dry sand on the table and blow gently. What happens to the pools of water? Do they blow about? Put a little water on a plate and blow gently. Why does the sand blow about and not the water? (Possibly they will suggest that the water is all stuck together whereas the sand is in little bits. Correct answers are not required. We are trying to provoke thought and discussion.)

4 Show the children how to make a cone from a paper circle by folding it and holding the folds in place with a paper clip.

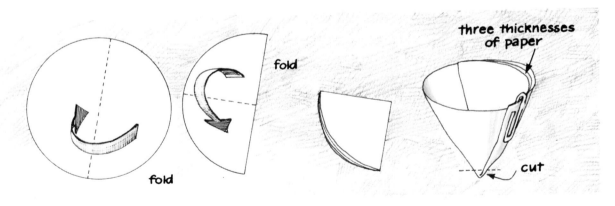

Show them how to cut off a very tiny piece at the point and then let them fill their cones with dry sand. They can enjoy trying to write their names or initials with the flowing sand.

Activity Sc3—Pebbles

Observing and investigating drainage and particle size

You need:

a collection of stones of different colours, with some rounded, and some angular and sharp; sand; soil; fine grit (as for a fish tank); five margarine cartons; five identical jam jars; five identical cups; a bowl of water; a small nail; a hammer; a magnifying glass.

1 Let the children put the stones into the bowl and wash them. What happens to the stones in the water? Do they float or sink? When the stones are clean, let the children spread them out on the table. Ask them to find stones which are the same colour and sort them into sets by colour. Look for ones which are a mixture of colours. Where will they put these? Encourage them to sort the stones by other qualities, either suggested by you or preferably by them as a result of their discussions. They may suggest rough/smooth, curved/angular. Suggest that they tap different pairs together to produce different sounds and that they find out which of a pair will scratch the other.

2 When they have finished looking at the stones, take a medium-sized stone and ask the children to put all those stones that are bigger on one side of the table and those that are smaller on the other side.

3 Now take the five margarine cartons and let the children see you make five holes in the bottom of each near the centre. Use the hammer and nail for this. Let them fill two cartons to 1 cm from the top: one with the bigger stones and one with the smaller ones.

4 Produce some grit and some sand and let the children rub them between their fingers. Can they tell you how they feel different and how they look different? They could also look at them through a magnifying glass. Encourage them to see that the grit is bigger and sharper than the sand and that it feels rougher. Fill a third carton with sand to the same mark and a fourth with grit. All the cartons should contain the same amount.

5 Next produce some fresh garden soil for the children to look at. They may find bits of twig, leaves, stones or live creatures. Encourage them to talk about what they find and get them to tell you how soil is different from sand in colour and texture. Fill the fifth carton with soil.

6 Balance each carton on top of a jam jar and ask the children what they think will happen if you pour a cupful of water into each carton. Let five children each fill a cup with water and then let each of them, at the same time, pour a cupful of water slowly into each of the cartons. Encourage them to watch carefully to decide which carton has the fastest drainage. Wait until the stones and grit have finished draining and put these in order, beginning with the fastest. Draw their attention to the amount of water in each jar. How is the water different? Is it clear or cloudy?

large pebbles   small pebbles   grit   sand   garden soil

7 Decide on a time to wait for the soil and the sand to drain, e.g. over lunch-time or until the end of the day, and then ask the children which jar has the most water in it. What does the water look like? Let them look at the sand and the soil. Can they tell you where the rest of the water is? Put them all in order now with labels: '1st–first', '2nd–second', and so on. You can also encourage them to talk about 'fastest', 'slowest', 'faster than' and 'slower than'.

8 Do they think that Rosa should make her pool in a gritty part of the beach or a sandy part?

Activity Sc4—Arm bands

Observing and investigating what air does

vestigating what air does

You need:

a water tray; an inflatable arm band; several clear plastic shampoo bottles; a small polythene bag; a bulldog clip; several pebbles or weights; some paper; scissors; sellotape; a bucket of water; each child needs a waterproof apron and a strip of paper 12 cm wide and 40 cm long.

1 Make sure that the arm band is completely empty and let the children feel it. Ask them what they think it is made of and why they think this. Encourage them to give reasons and evidence for their own ideas. Ask them about its colour and its shape. Stand it on its end so that the children can see that it is a short cylinder. Give each of them a strip of paper and ask them first of all to make a tall cylinder and then a short cylinder. Get them now to sellotape their short cylinders and fold them flat like the arm band.

2 Now inflate the arm band and discuss how it changes shape. Let the children feel it and describe it; they should notice that it has changed from being flat to being curved.

3 Put the inflated arm band in the water and let the children see that it floats. Ask them to push it under water. What happens? Can they think of a way of making the arm band sink? Try some of their suggestions and then attach a polythene bag of pebbles with a bulldog clip. What happens? Discuss the fact that one of these arm bands on each arm will keep a person afloat. (Better still, visit the swimming baths and demonstrate this.)

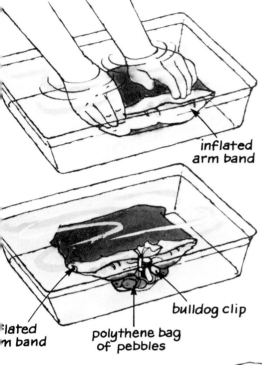

inflated arm band

bulldog clip

lated n band

polythene bag of pebbles

air bubbles

empty shampoo bottle

air bubble   water

4 Now ask them what you did to change the shape of the arm band from flat to curved. Get them to pretend that they are blowing up arm bands. If they put their hands in front of their mouths, what do they feel? (They will feel the breath coming from their mouths.) Can they see the breath? Have they ever seen it?

5 Ask again what is inside the arm band. Ask them how you got the breaths to put into the arm band. Pretend to blow it up again and make sure that they realise that you gulped in air and then blew it into the arm band. Show them how you can empty the arm band and do this under water, so that the children can see the bubbles of air.

6 Now put the flat arm band in the water and ask the children what it is doing. Get them to press it under water. Is it easier or harder to press under water now that it is not blown up? Is it easier to make it sink? Let them try various methods and then once more attach the bag of pebbles. Ask them why the flat arm bands would not be any good for keeping somebody afloat.

7 Now give them the empty shampoo bottles with their tops on. Encourage the children to talk about the different shapes. Are they flat or curved? Let them float their bottles in the water. Get them to push the bottles under the water. What happens? If they push them right down to the bottom of the bucket of water and then let go suddenly, what happens? Ask them what is in the bottles. If they say, 'Nothing' or that they are empty, suggest that they take the tops off under water and see what happens. What do they see? What has come out of the bottles? What has gone into their bottles?

8 Let them fill their bottles completely with water and put the tops on. Suggest that they turn their bottles upside down. Have any of the bottles got bubbles inside them? Can the children make the bubble go to the bottom? What is the bubble made of? Can they think of a way of getting rid of the bubble? Help them to see that they must put more water in to take the place of the bubble.

9 Finally, ask the children what they think will happen if they put their bottles full of water into the bowl of water or the bucket of water. Let them try and see if they are right. Do the bottles float as easily as when they had air in them? Is it easy to sink them? Can they tell you that air if it is enclosed can help to keep you afloat?

10 If you go to the swimming baths, you can show the children how air can be trapped in wet clothing and keep people afloat. This is important in life-saving drill and is one of the things the lifeguard needs to know and be able to do.

Activity Sc5—Drying

Investigating what happens when air blows on wet things

You need:

a hand-held hair dryer with guard; a bowl of water; several towels of different kinds and thicknesses; paper kitchen towels; two jam jars; cling film; rubber bands.

1 Get the children to talk about how they get dry when they have been swimming. What does it feel like when you come out of the water? Do you feel warm or cold? What do you do to get dry?

2 Produce a bowl of water and your collection of towels. Ask two or three of the children to wet their hands and to describe what they look like and what they feel like. This is a good opportunity to point out that our skin does not get wet all over but that the water forms drips and blobs. Has anyone any ideas why? Has anyone seen anything like that before? (e.g. Fat on hands?) Now ask the children to choose one of the towels to dry their hands. What do their hands look like now? Where has the water gone? Does the towel feel wet now? What does the towel feel like when we have used it after we have been swimming (even if it has not been dropped in a puddle)? Would it feel wet? What do we do to get the towel dry again? Let the children hang their towel up to dry.

3 Ask the children if they have ever been anywhere where they do not provide towels for drying hands but hot air dryers. Tell them that you have a hair dryer and they can see if that will dry their hands. Let them each wet one of their hands and then use the dryer on 'warm' to dry them.

Tell them to watch very carefully what happens to the water. Where does it go? Let them wet their other hands and then dry them with the dryer on 'cold'. What happens this time? What does it feel like? What does it feel like when you blow cold air on a dry hand? Does it feel the same as with the cold air on a wet hand? How does it feel different? Does cold air dry your hand more quickly than warm air or more slowly? Where does the cold air make the water go to? Encourage the children to talk about all these experiences. They should understand that the water goes into the air. No more is necessary at this stage.

4 Tell the children that you are going to set a puzzle for them. Take two paper kitchen towels, wet them evenly, squeeze them so that they are not dripping and loosely put one into each of the jam jars. Cover the top of one jar with cling film, held in place with a rubber band. Now ask the children which piece of kitchen paper will dry first – or will there not be any difference? Can they guess? Can they give reasons for their guesses?

5 Let them look at the jars at intervals and see what happens. Draw their attention to the appearance of the cling film. What is on the underside of it? Where has it come from? Where is it going? (Water has evaporated in the jar but is unable to escape. It condenses on the cling film.) When the towel in the open jar is dry you can look at the piece which has been in the other jar and discover that it is still wet. Why? (The water could not get into the air. There was no room for it in the air in the jar.) Did they guess right? (It is good if they did, but if they did not they have all the time in the world!)

Activity Sc6—Ice lollies

Investigating freezing and melting

You need:
a bottle of orange concentrate; a large clear glass or plastic jug; a cup; a glass; a long-handled spoon; an ice-making tray of cubes; a plastic tray from a chocolate box; cocktail sticks; two clear differently shaped small jugs; access to the freezing compartment of a refrigerator. (The quantities of liquid used will depend on the relative sizes of your containers. See instructions below.)

1 Ask one of the children to pour two cupfuls of water into the large glass jug. Check each time that the cup is full to the brim. Encourage the children to talk about pouring and splashing, dripping and all the other things that water does and what it looks like. You can use the word 'liquid' and associate it with these properties.

2 Next, let one of the children measure a cupful of orange concentrate. Again emphasise its liquid properties and use the word 'liquid' to describe it. Emphasise that both water and orange concentrate do the same things and this is why we can call them both liquids. Talk about how the concentrate is different from water – in colour, taste, transparency and thickness.

3 Now, pour just a little of the concentrate into the water in the jug. Ask the children to describe what happens. It should be clear at the top and orange coloured at the bottom. Stir it and ask again what happens. What colour is it now? Can you still see through it?

4 Add the rest of the concentrate, stir the mixture and discuss the way in which it has changed from pale orange to deep orange, and has become all the same colour.

5 Fill each of the smaller jugs to the brim with the diluted orange and ask the children which jug they think will hold more. Get them to talk about the different ways they might find out.

Which holds more?

How many can you fill?

Ice lollies

6 Suggest that while they are making ice lollies they can compare the sizes of the jugs. Let one of the children find out how many cubes he or she can fill from one of the jugs, while another child works with the other jug. Ask each child how many ice cubes are filled. Which jug is bigger?

7 How many cubes have they filled? How many cocktail sticks will they need? Let the children put the sticks in place. Do they go in easily?

8 Look at the shapes inside the chocolate box mould and pour in the remainder of the orange mixture. Put in the sticks. Ask the children what will happen if you put the liquid in the freezer. What shape will each ice shape be and what will happen to the sticks? Put all the things in the freezer until they are frozen.

9 When you take them out, ask what has happened to the sticks. Can they get the sticks out? Can they move them about? Is the mixture a liquid any more? Let them prod the ice and realise that its properties are quite different from those of a liquid. You can use the word 'solid' to describe this state.

10 Give them each an ice lolly to enjoy. Discuss the shape, the taste, the colour and the temperature. Is it colder than the inside of their mouth or not? How does it feel?

11 Give the children the ice shapes from the chocolate box mould. Ask how they are different from the lollies. Suggest that they hold the ice shapes in their hands. What happens to them? What makes the solid turn to liquid? How does it feel? How do they know that it is a liquid that is forming?

12 If they want to keep their chocolate box shapes solid, that is, they do not want them to melt, where would be a good place to put them? Where would they put them if they want them to melt quickly?

13 Tell the children that you have another puzzle for them. Produce a glass of water and pick up one of the chocolate box ice shapes. Ask them what will happen if you put it in the water. Will it float or sink? Will it stay as it is or will something happen to it?

Activity Sc7—Wheels

Investigating what happens when wheels turn

alk mark

chalk mark

chalk marks

You need:
a tricycle; a quoit; a hoop; round tins; round cheese boxes; cotton reels; toy car wheels; chalk; a large sheet of paper; felt-tipped pens.

1 Let a child sit on the tricycle with his or her feet on the pedals. Tell the child to make the tricycle go forwards and then backwards. Ask the children what the rider is doing to make it move. Tell the child to push gently on the pedals and let the other children watch what is happening to the wheels. Help them to see that the wheels turn on a spindle and that the spindle slowly moves forward (as does the tricycle).

2 When the tricycle is still, put a chalk mark on the wheel and a matching one on the floor. Now let the child pedal very slowly forward and ask the other children to watch the chalk mark on the wheel. Which way is it going? When the wheel has revolved once, mark the floor again. Now ask the child to go slowly backwards until the marks match again.

3 Have the hoop and quoit ready and ask the children what shape they are. Which is the bigger circle? Mark the hoop and the quoit with chalk and arrange a starting line on the floor. Match the chalk mark on the hoop with the starting line and push the hoop forward to make one revolution. Make a chalk mark on the floor at this point.

4 Now look at the quoit and ask the children where they think it will reach in one complete turn. Do they think it will go further than the hoop or not as far? Mark the quoit and try it. Were the children right?

one
revolution

5 Put out your collection of round items and ask the children how they are the same. Encourage them to see that they all have circles in them and that they will all roll.

6 Give the children a large sheet of paper and mark a starting line. Tell the children to mark the rim of each of the round objects and show them again how to match the rim mark with the starting line. Let the children find out how far each of the objects goes in one revolution. Ask them which circle they think will go the furthest and which the shortest distance. Why do they think this? Let them find the distance for each object. Were they right?

7 They could make a display of a set of objects which will roll and a set which will not.

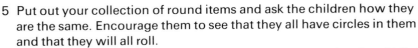

Activity Sc8—On the level

Investigating level

You need:

a clear polythene bottle for each child; rubber bands; a tray; a bowl; a large clear coffee jar; cookery colouring; a ball; plasticine.

1 Tell the children to look at the floor and ask them whether it is level o sloping. Put a ball on the floor and watch what happens. Ask the children what would happen if the floor was sloping.
2 Use the tray and a book to make a gentle slope and put the ball on th slope. What happens to the ball? Which way does it roll?
3 Now ask them what would happen to water on a slope. Lay the tray and put a little water on it. Wedge it up slightly with a small lump of plasticine under one end. What happens to the water? Which way do it go?
4 Half fill the bowl with water and tilt it gently. Ask the children what would happen if the bowl was on a steep slope.
5 Put the ball on the table. What happens? Can the children tell you whether or not the table is level?
6 Now half fill the coffee jar with coloured water and put it on the level table. Put a rubber band round it to mark the water level. Let the children make sure that it is in the correct place. Put the jar on the sloping tray and let the children gently alter the slope of the tray, watching what happens to the water level in the jar. Where does the tray have to be for the rubber band to mark the water level accurately Let the children investigate until they are satisfied that the tray must level.
7 Give each of the children a bottle containing some coloured water an a rubber band and let each of them set up a level-finding bottle. Let them investigate surfaces in the classroom and in the school to see if they are level. (You could stage-manage a few examples.)

rubber band

coloured water

Making and doing activities

The problem for the child is:
'Can you make a model tent?'

You need:

small garden canes; string; sellotape; rubber bands; scrap cloth; paper various kinds; plastic sheet (carrier bags); paint; plasticine.

Encourage the children to tackle the problem systematically and talk about it before they start.

1 The problem   Can you make a model tent?

2 Exploring the problem

What is a tent? What does a tent have to do? What do people use tents for? If it was a real tent what would the cover have to do? What would the frame have to do? How do other people make tents? What do they make them from? (Pictures and information about tents of all kinds, ranging from nomadic tents to illustrations in modern catalogues, can be collected.)

3 Ideas for solving the problem

You might like to guide the children towards a simple cone shaped tent if they are not more ambitious.

4 Making

It is very difficult to judge the amount of material required to cover a frame: it always takes more than expected. Help them to make some simple estimates. Once they have managed to produce a cover for the frame, they may like to decorate it.

5 Evaluating

The children can talk about their models and ask questions about them, e.g. 'What would happen to the people in your tent if it rained or if the wind blew?' 'How do people get in and out?'

You can have a display of tents and include it in a wider study of tents.

Further activities

Some suggestions

1 Find out what happens to damp sand when it is frozen.
2 Let the children blow up balloons, preferably by mouth (to appreciate the effort involved) but otherwise with a balloon pump. What happens when you let go of an inflated balloon? Why?
3 Make jam sandwiches. Leave one out on the plate and put another in a plastic bag. What happens?
4 Grow cress. Use it to make a sandwich to eat.
5 Make pictures of safe places to play during the holidays, e.g. garden, park.
6 Make a collection of shells. What are shells? (They used to be homes of animals.)
7 Use pictures to time-sequence for a day out.

EXTENSIONS

Introduction

In the very early stages of developing *Longman Scienceworld*, it was recognised that there were areas of concern to which particular attention should be given. As a result of this, a series of guiding principles was drawn up, and this is set out below.

Principles

About science
1 Science is a way of looking at the world which is unique and therefore different from the view of the world provided by other disciplines.
2 Being able to look at the world scientifically requires the development of particular skills, abilities and attitudes.
3 By looking at the world in this way, a body of scientific knowledge has been produced.
4 Science is a major contributor to technological development.
5 Science is used in society in all sorts of ways. People use it in their work and hobbies. Everyone is confronted with it in everyday life.

About science for young children
6 Science for young children is an active process, which requires the development of those skills, abilities and attitudes which will enable them to explore their surroundings in a scientific way.
7 The scheme concerns itself with ideas and information – with scientific knowledge – because the children themselves will acquire ideas and information, as a consequence of their own active exploration of their surroundings. This information and these ideas will be relevant to the children since they will be the children's own.
8 It is probable that the information and ideas will be concerned with the immediate environment because that will be the context of most of the children's active exploration. Equally, if we are concerned to develop children's ability to work scientifically, it is likely that things and actions in the close environment will be most effective in arousing children's interest and encouraging their active involvement.
9 A particular scientific idea can be introduced in a wide variety of contexts. Scientific investigation and activity can be concerned with a wide range of subjects. It is, therefore, necessary to establish criteria for selecting contexts. The contexts chosen here reflect the following concerns:
   – interest for the children;
   – compatibility with the whole curriculum – the contexts must fit the normal curriculum pattern;
   – potential for the development of scientific skills;
   – provision of a wide range of experiences across the sciences;
   – provision of experiences of some major areas of understanding, e.g. life processes, energy conversion, etc;
   – potential for showing how a scientific perspective is useful and is relevant in a variety of circumstances – in everyday life, in jobs and in hobbies.
10 It is very important that children should develop an understanding of the relationship between science and technology. They should be provided with opportunities to engage in simple problem-solving activities. Working towards the solution of a problem is valuable in its own right; at the same time, it provides many opportunities for scientific investigation, and enables children to bring together their developing skills and abilities not only in science but also in other disciplines.
11 Evidence furnished by Piaget and others suggests that there is to some extent a developmental pattern which most children follow. This should be taken into account, but the scientific activities proposed should encourage development rather than just provide a passive response to this developmental pattern.

About teachers and science

12 The form of *Longman Scienceworld* and its classroom approach should be compatible with the normal patterns of organisation used by teachers in primary schools.

13 Many teachers feel that they have had little experience of science in their own education and believe that they do not have a solid enough basis from which to teach it. This science scheme should help these teachers to overcome their doubts and provide the information and encouragement necessary to give them the confidence to introduce science into the curriculum.

14 Teaching science involves careful attention to classroom organisation. The materials should provide the teacher with adequate guidance and advice.

15 Science has great potential for providing opportunities and stimuli for the development of language and the application of mathematics. These opportunities should be exploited.

16 Following children's progress in acquiring scientific skills and abilities is an important aspect of ensuring that children are given systematic help in developing their skills and abilities. Particular attention should be paid, therefore, to recording progress.

Some of these principles have been expanded to present a more detailed framework. They follow in the form of Extensions A–J.

Extension A   Scientific skills

Science for children in the primary school is essentially about observing, investigating and making sense of the world. The intention of *Longman Scienceworld* is to provide children with opportunities to carry out these investigations and to foster the development of the necessary skills, abilities and attitudes.

First, it must be made clear that 'investigating' is not the same as 'experimenting' as conventionally used in describing scientific activity. Our investigating differs from experimenting in a way which is best made clear diagramatically. In essence, conventional science works like this:

Diagram 1

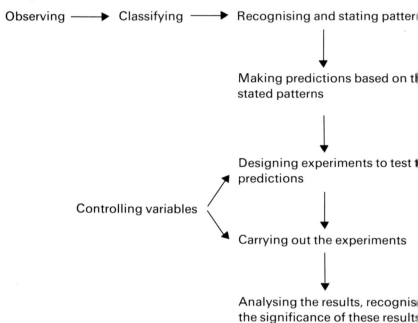

Observing ⟶ Classifying ⟶ Recognising and stating patterns

Making predictions based on the stated patterns

Designing experiments to test the predictions

Controlling variables

Carrying out the experiments

Analysing the results, recognising the significance of these results

Opinions differ about the order of the early stages of this sequence but it remains that experimenting is about careful planned testing of a formally stated prediction based on a formally stated recognition of a pattern. This sequence involves a high level of understanding and the ability to manipulate and communicate ideas. In the planning of experiments, it is necessary to be able to recognise and plan the control of a range of variables. Again, this involves thinking in a highly sophisticated way.

Manipulation of ideas at this level is inappropriate for most children of primary school age (and indeed for many older children). It is probably the complexity of thinking which is implied in this approach to science that has led to the non-acceptance of a number of primary science curriculum developments.

What then is meant by 'investigating'? Firstly, some investigations are an extension of observing. Instead of just observing what is, the child carries out some action and finds out what happens when . . ., or what happens if . . . . Observing the sound when an object is tapped, planting seeds, or adding water to salt are investigations at this simple level. An event is provoked and what happens is observed. No prediction is being tested but observation is being directed towards looking for some change. (Simple observation is concerned with observing what is there. No change is provoked although a change may be observed, e.g. change in nature.)

At this simple level of investigation, no attempt may be made to recognise or control variables. The investigation is concerned with what happens on a particular occasion. The investigation requires planning; the results are observed, communicated and recorded. Measurement may be involved and there will be discussion of what is observed. It is the nature of this discussion which will probably determine what happens next. Children may be content with the information they have acquired or, with encouragement, they may begin to frame questions of the sort, 'If that was what happened when we did that, I wonder what would happen if we did this?' It is this kind of thinking which leads to a more refined pattern of investigation, which can best be described diagramatically.

Diagram 2

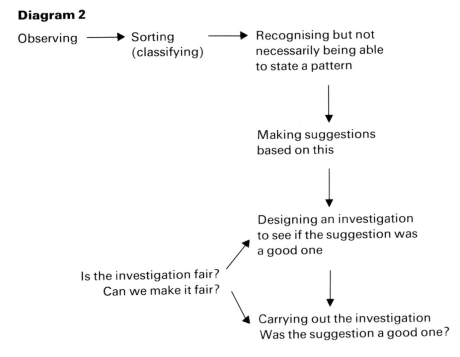

This differs significantly from the statement about experimenting in Diagram 1. Children are not expected to be able to make formal statements of patterns, or recognise and control a range of variables. Expectations are pitched lower and chances of success are greater. Progress to the more formal sequence of experimenting may develop over the years. The objective is to help children to develop the skills needed at a pace which is possible for them. It must be realised that being able to recognise and state a pattern of behaviour or being able to recognise and plan the control of a range of variables is a complex task. Some children of primary school age will possess the required degree of maturity but many will need a good deal of help. Nevertheless, many children will, on occasion, show an understanding which is apparently out of phase with their general level of development. This should be noted with pleasure but great care should be exercised in assessing its significance. *Longman Scienceworld* helps children to develop the skills required to carry out investigations. The sophistication of the methods they use will increase as their skills mature.

In the early part of the scheme, the prime concern is to develop the skills of observing and communicating information about what is observed. Measuring is introduced as a refinement of both observing and communicating. Recording and classifying are other skills which are introduced at an early stage. Recognising and describing patterns is recognised as a high level skill which will be developed gradually from the simple standpoint described in Diagram 2. Again, the skill of predicting will be developed by starting with the idea of good suggestions – although for the sake of simplicity and lack of a more appropriate word, the word 'predicting' will be used for 'making a good suggestion'. Controlling variables is another skill to be developed within the limits described, concentrating largely on the idea of making investigations fair.

Development of the skills needed to carry out scientific investigations is brought about in two distinct ways. In some of the suggested activities, one or two particular skills are considered in isolation, e.g. observing or sorting. In other activities, an investigation is suggested that requires a range of skills to be used and developed.

Table 1 overleaf describes the development of skills in the primary years in *Longman Scienceworld*.

Table 1 Development of the science skills

	Children starting the scheme	Children at the end of the infant years	Children at the end of the junior years
Observing	The children can observe using the senses individually as suggested by the teacher. They can compare simple objects.	The children can observe using the senses in combination, aided by a range of measures and magnifiers and over a period of time (change, behaviour, etc.). The most appropriate observations to make are determined by the children prompted by the teacher. The children can, in retrospect, identify the most appropriate observations.	The children can observe using the senses in combination aided by a range of measures and magnifiers used with skill and over a period of time (change, behaviour, etc.). The children can decide which will be the most appropriate observations to make.
Communicating	The children can communicate in simple oral statements assisted by the teacher's prompts.	The children can communicate in detail using a range of methods. In retrospect, they are able to choose the most appropriate from a number of possible methods tried.	The children can communicate in detail using a refined range of methods and can choose for themselves the most appropriate method to use.
Measuring	The children can compare two objects placed side by side.	The children can measure using a range of equipment including some standard measures. They can exercise judgement about the level of accuracy/approximation which is appropriate. They can measure with precision.	The children can measure using a range of equipment. They can use their own judgement about what should be measured and how accurately the measurement should be made.
Recording	Some children can record by simple picture or mathematical representation.	The children can record using a wide range of methods including mathematical representation. With prompting they can choose retrospectively, from a number of methods tried, the most appropriate for a particular purpose.	The children can record using a wide range of methods including mathematical representation. They can choose in advance the most appropriate method for a particular purpose.
Classifying	The children can classify according to one characteristic suggested by the teacher.	The children can classify into sets and subsets using complex criteria if prompted by the teacher.	The children can classify into sets and subsets using complex criteria selected by themselves. They can use and construct simple keys.
Recognising patterns	The concept is not appreciated.	When making observations, the children may seek patterns if prompted by the teacher. They can recognise common factors in the information obtained by observing a number of instances. They are not able to describe the pattern formally. They may or may not be able to identify other instances which fit the pattern.	When making observations, the children seek patterns in the information obtained. They recognise common factors in the information obtained by observing a number of instances. They are able to recognise other instances which fit the pattern.
Predicting	The children make suggestions, guesses or predictions based indiscriminately on experience and fantasy.	The children make reasonable suggestions based on observations which may be carried out over a period of time. Some causal relationships are recognised.	The children base their suggestions on firm evidence including recognised patterns. There is increasing recognition of causal as distinct from casual relationships. They use known concepts in making suggestions.
Controlling variables	There is little appreciation of the existence of variables, and minimal recognition of causal relationships.	The children start to identify one or two obvious variables. These may or may not be relevant. The children are able to find out whether or not they are relevant. When a variable is identified, the children are able to find a way of controlling it if prompted by the teacher.	The children are aware of a wide range of variables and can, on most occasions identify and control those which are relevant.
Investigating	With clear directions from the teacher, the children can carry out and understand simple investigations.	The children may suggest what they would like to investigate or test. They can design and carry out simple investigations with only minimal help with practicalities. They start to notice the more obvious variables and can suggest ways of testing whether they are relevant. With some help, the children can control one or two of the variables they have identified.	The children can design and carry out simple investigations with confidence. They can identify and control most relevant variables. They can review the investigations critically and check results by repetition.

Each of these skills will be developed in a structured way through the scheme. This step by step progression is set out in Table 2 which follows. The table not only indicates the stage of development of the skills in the work at the different levels, but it also provides a guide as to what the children should be able to do when they have completed the work of a particular level. It should be noted that in going from one level to the next, the skills are cumulative and the skills taught at each level build on those acquired earlier.

The *Record Sheets* for *Longman Scienceworld* which are available separately are based on this table of skill development.

Table 2 is in two parts. Table 2(i) covers the infant years and Table 2(ii) covers the junior years. Both parts are included here so that teachers of infants may see the progression through the junior years of those skills which are being developed in the infant years.

Table 2(i)   The infant years

	Year 1		Year 2	
	Level 1	**Level 2**	**Level 1**	**Level 2**
Observing	The children can observe differences and similarities using the senses individually as specified by the teacher. One attribute at a time is observed and direct comparisons are made.	The children can observe using more than one sense and can cope with more than one attribute. Observations are still immediate and teacher prompted.	The children choose appropriate senses to observe changes, behaviour and movement. Arbitrary measures are used to refine observation.	The children can observe movement in relation to time. They are able to select increasingly appropriate arbitrary measures and start see some need for standard measures.
Communicating	The children can make simple oral statements describing and naming in terms of one property. They can use pictorial representation suggested by the teacher. They ask questions.	The children use more accurate oral descriptions for more than one property. Sets can be described pictorially.	The children can include in their oral descriptions the time sequence of events related to change. They can use a very simple block graph as a means of communication.	The children can now exten their oral descriptions to include comments on result They can make statements and justify these with reaso They can use block graphs and pictorial representation more freely.
Measuring	The children can describe length and weight orally. They can make direct comparison of unequal lengths and use their hands to compare unequal weights directly. They can describe capacity (non-relative). They can time-sequence in simple fashion.	The children can match objects of the same length or use several objects to make up the length. They can decide whether containers hold more or less by judgement and by counting. Weighing and time sequence are as at level 1.	The children can measure length using repeated units and limb measures. They can use balance scales to balance and order weights. They can compare capacity by emptying or filling. They can compare fast and slow.	Length, weight and capacit are as at level 1. The childre are now able to measure tim e.g. with an egg timer.
Recording	The children can make classroom displays of sets by grouping actual objects. They can use simple pictorial representation and show relationships using arrows provided by the teacher.	The children can use simple tallying and pictorial representation. They can match words and sentences to appropriate sets. The recording method is suggested by the teacher.	The children can use simple charts relating to behaviour and movement. They are able to indicate by ticking in appropriate columns. They can use double-ended arrows for balances etc. and simple graphs. They are able to do their own drawings and copy simple sentences. The method of recording is suggested by the teacher.	The children are able to writ their own sentences, use greater than and less than signs, and use a simple mat They exploit their improved accuracy in drawing and cutting out. If the teacher suggests two methods of recording, the children are able after discussion to choose the more appropriat
Classifying	The children can sort for one attribute by matching an example provided by the teacher.	The children can sort for two attributes decided by the teacher; if the teacher sorts, the children can identify the criteria being used.	The children are able to suggest more than one way of sorting a given collection and decide their own criteria. Sorting criteria may include purpose, movement and behaviour if these are identified by the teacher.	The children can sort according to the properties materials using very simple keys. They are able to notic and match several common features of different materia
Recognising patterns	The children are unlikely to be able to appreciate the idea.		The children are now better able to recognise similarities and describe these.	With prompting, the childr can look for patterns in the observations.
Predicting	The children can suggest what will happen next. There is some evidence that the suggestions are based on experience, but reality and fantasy overlap considerably.		The children can make reasonable suggestions about likely outcomes based on the observations made in the course of ar activity.	
Controlling variables	The children generally have little appreciation of the variables. The teacher controls the variables by providing restricted sets of materials and guiding investigations.		The children generally have little appreciation of the variables. The teacher controls the variables by providing restricted sets of materials and guiding investigations.	If the teacher suggests that variable may be affecting th outcome of an investigatio the children may or may no recognise this as significan
Investigating	The teacher can set a problem of the 'What happens when . . .?' type. The teacher provides a restricted set of materials and suggests the method. The children are able to carry out the investigation and make the necessary observations.		The teacher can suggest a problem. The children make suggestions about approaches and solve some of the practical problems. They need support and guidance and practical help. The teacher draws attention to related features but does not refer directly to cause and effect.	In the practical design of th investigation, more than on method may be tried by the children and a comparison made. The children begin t notice related features and some will recognise cause effect relationships. Investigations include 'Wh is best?' as well as 'What happens when . . .?'

Year 3

	Level 1	Level 2
serving	The children can make observations at different times which are related to each other in sequence, so that they are able to observe gradual changes. They can use some standard measures to refine observations.	The children can make judgements about the level of detail and accuracy needed in their observations. They can appreciate to some extent the concept of approximation. They can increase the accuracy of their observations by using standard measures. In retrospect, they can choose which observations are most appropriate for the task.
mmunicating	The children can make detailed observations orally and can express their reasons for choices. They can produce simple written accounts including mathematical representation and, orally, they can discuss the appropriateness of the means of communicating which they have used.	Orally, the children are able to give a detailed account of what was done and why, what happened and in what order. They can take part in a discussion of their results and draw some conclusions. Their written communications are increasingly appropriate.
asuring	The children appreciate the need for a standard measure and can use the metre. They can now weigh, using $\frac{1}{2}$ kg and kg. They can balance against gram weights. Capacity and time are as at year 2, level 2.	The children can measure using rods marked in cm and 10 cm. They can measure straight and curved lines. They can weigh using grams, measure capacity in litres and half litres, and can calculate time intervals.
cording	The children are able to record some measurements by using more detailed graphs. They are able to produce their own representational and observational drawings. They are able to attempt their own written records and can record over a longer period of time, noting and interpreting development. If the teacher suggests methods of recording, the children are able to comment on the usefulness of these and decide which to use.	The children's ability to draw proportions more accurately and to match colours more precisely is used in recording; this reflects their increasingly precise and accurate observational skills. Written accounts are more detailed and orderly, and records can be kept competently over a period of time. The children can suggest different methods of recording and use these. In retrospect, with prompting, they can choose which was the most suitable method and give reasons for their choice.
ssifying	The children can sort into sets and subsets. Sorting criteria may include characteristics of plants and animals.	The children can sort using more complex and less evident criteria. They can use simple keys.
ognising terns	The children can now recognise patterns. They will probably not be able to describe the pattern formally. They may or may not be able to identify other examples which fit the pattern.	
dicting	The children can make reasonable suggestions based on observations over a period of time. They can recognise some causal relationships.	
trolling iables	If the teacher suggests one variable, the children can discuss its implications and test whether it is or is not affecting the outcome of the investigation.	The children start to identify one or two variables. These will not always be relevant but the children will be able to investigate their relevance. When a relevant variable has been identified, the children should be able to find a way of controlling it.
estigating	The children make useful suggestions about the design of investigations and carry them out with help. The teacher suggests one variable and the children can find out whether or not it affects the outcome. The children see more cause and effect relationships if the teacher points out related features which the children have not noticed.	The children may suggest what they would like to investigate. They design and carry out investigations with minimal help with practicalities. They start to notice one or two more obvious variables and with help can suggest methods of controlling these. They can carry out an agreed controlled investigation.

Table 2(ii)   The junior years

	Year 1		Year 2	
	Level 1	**Level 2**	**Level 1**	**Level 2**
Observing	The children can observe using the senses in combination, aided by a range of measures and magnifiers and over a period of time. They are able to observe change, behaviour, etc. as well as the more obvious features, such as colour. The most appropriate observations are determined by the children, prompted by the teacher. The children can make judgements about the level of detail and accuracy needed in their observations. They can appreciate the concept of approximation to some extent. They can increase the accuracy of their observations by using standard measures. In retrospect, they can choose which observations are most appropriate for the task.	The children are increasingly able to observe detail. Independently, they recognise in advance that some observations may be of more significance than others.	With prompting, the children will seek to observe in detail and will select the appropriate equipment to do this. They are able to suggest in advance that certain observations may be of greater significance than others. With some prompting, they are able to view a sequence of observations as a whole.	Without prompting, the children observe in detail w accuracy. They can select in advance which observation to make and begin to observ for purpose, e.g. they look fo similarities and differences i form.
Communicating	The children can communicate in detail using a range of methods, including mathematical ones. In retrospect, they are able to choose the most appropriate from a number of methods tried. Orally, the children are able to give a detailed account of what was done and why, what happened and in what order. They can take part in a discussion of their results and draw some conclusions. Their written communications are increasingly appropriate.	The children can give clearer accounts of their work both orally and in writing. Their oral work is more confident, and after discussion they can choose an appropriate form of written communication. With prompting, they include mathematical communication of various kinds among the methods of communication which they consider.	The children are able to communicate in detail, which parallels the increasing detail they are able to observe. With prompting, they are able to suggest different methods of communication, and after discussion will choose an appropriate method. They include mathematical communication among the methods they consider as a matter of course.	The children's ability to communicate develops in parallel with a more sophisticated approach to observing and investigating Orally, the children are able explain the plans and decisions which they make prior to and during observation and investigatio They can state their plan clearly. They can write a clea detailed account of their observations and investigations. They choose mathematical means of communication as appropriate.
Measuring	When directed, the children are able to use an appropriate measuring instrument. Length, Weight, Capacity – comparative, arbitrary, and standard measures where appropriate: metres and half metres, kilograms and half kilograms, litres and half litres Time – intervals of time using timers and stop clocks Temperature – using a thermometer with easy-to-read scale	The children can measure using the most appropriate measuring instrument for the task within the limits of their conceptual understanding of quantity. Length – metres and centimetres Weight – kilograms and parts of kilogram Capacity – litres and parts of litre	The children can measure using the most appropriate measuring instrument within the limits of their conceptual understanding of quantity and can measure to finer limits. Length – metres and centimetres Weight – kilograms and grams Capacity – millilitres (multiples of 10) Time – minutes and parts of a minute	The children can measure to finer degree of accuracy usir the most appropriate measuring instrument. They can attempt to decide what measure. Length – metres and centimetres Weight – kilograms and gran Capacity – millilitres (multiples of 10) Time – minutes and seconds
Recording	The children can record using a wide range of methods, including mathematical representation. They are able to draw in more detail and with more accuracy. Written records are more detailed and orderly and can be maintained over a period of time. The children can suggest different methods of recording and use these. In retrospect and with prompting, they can choose which was the most suitable and give reasons for their choice.	The children extend the range of recording methods which they use. They can write short accounts, and suggest the use of tables and block graphs which they construct with help. With prompting, they can consider in retrospect their success in recording.	The children are able to make notes and write a clear account based on these notes. They are able to record a sequence of events. They attempt to choose the most appropriate recording method in advance and for a simple record can proceed independently. They use tables, block graphs and diagrams.	The children begin to consid more carefully in advance th recording method(s) which will be most appropriate for the task in hand. With help, they make a choice and can then proceed.

	Year 3		Year 4	
	Level 1	**Level 2**	**Level 1**	**Level 2**
Observing	The children can identify which observations are likely to be significant and can make these in detail. They make less significant observations in less detail. In embarking on a sequence of observations, they are able to decide which observations are likely to be significant without prompting. They observe for purpose, e.g. they look for similarities and differences in form and behaviour. With prompting, they notice patterns in form and behaviour.	The children are increasingly able to make decisions about what to observe and in what detail to make the observations. They look for similarities and differences in form and behaviour. They look for change and can observe it in detail. With prompting, they observe patterns of behaviour and change.	They are able independently to select which observations are likely to be significant and make these in appropriate detail. They look for similarities and differences in form and behaviour. They look for, and are increasingly able to discern, patterns in their observations of form, behaviour and change.	The children can observe using the senses in combination. They can observe in detail. They can distinguish in advance between more and less significant observations, determine the level of detail which will be appropriate and make their observations accordingly. They look for and observe similarities and differences; with some prompting, they recognise observational patterns of form, behaviour and change, as well as of more obvious qualities such as colour.
Communicating	The children appreciate more clearly that the communications should be suited to the audience for whom they are intended. With help both orally and in writing, they can produce different kinds of communication and, in retrospect, can decide which would be suitable for an identified audience.	With prompting, the children can attempt to match the communication to the identified audience. They are able to describe their investigations and observations clearly and sequentially.	Without prompting, the children attempt to match their communications to the audience. They are able to describe and discuss their observations and the observational patterns they discern. They are increasingly able to convey clear statements about these observational patterns. With help, they can make suggestions connected with these recognised patterns.	The children can communicate in detail, using a refined range of methods, and can choose for themselves the most appropriate method to use.
Measuring	The children can read and record using decimalisation. Length – metres and centimetres, e.g. 1.32 m Weight – kilograms and grams, e.g. 1.250 kg Capacity – litres and millilitres, e.g. 1.625 l They can read scales and dials after selecting the appropriate measuring instrument for the task. They can read different calibrations on a variety of instruments.	The children can select the most appropriate instrument to give an accurate reading, e.g. force meter, spring balance, stopwatch, etc. They can read these instruments competently.	The children can measure, using their own judgement about what should be measured. With guidance, they can decide how accurate the measurement should be.	The children are able to use appropriate standard measures with confidence: (m, cm, mm, cm², cm³, kg, g, l, ml, min, sec, newton). They can record using decimal notation. They can estimate with a reasonable degree of accuracy. They can select the appropriate measuring instrument to suit a particular purpose and read a variety of scales, e.g. thermometer, kitchen scales (both dial and linear), force meter and spring balance.
Recording	The children plan their recording method(s) in advance and include methods such as flow charts, block graphs and tables. They write accurate notes and produce a detailed orderly account. They can consider their efforts critically but may need prompting to act accordingly.	They give increasing consideration to mathematical recording methods and with help use a widening range. They draw and colour more accurately. They begin to consider for whom the record is intended and become aware that different recording methods may be appropriate for different audiences, e.g. self, teacher, other children.	The children plan their recording method(s) in advance, including the recording of a series of events over time. They can keep an observational diary and write an orderly sequenced account from this. They can consider critically the record which they have produced and suggest how it might be improved.	The children can record using a wide range of methods, including mathematical representation. They can choose in advance the most appropriate method for a particular purpose.

	Year 1		Year 2	
	Level 1	**Level 2**	**Level 1**	**Level 2**
Classifying	The children can classify into sets and subsets, using complex criteria if prompted by the teacher. They are able independently to sort, using simple criteria. They can use keys for simple criteria and, with help, for more complex criteria.	The children are aware that there are different criteria for sorting which could be used. Using simple criteria they are able to sort in different ways. With help, they extend the range of criteria to include, for example, behaviour and origin. With help, they can construct keys using simple criteria.	The children can confidently sort in different ways, using simple criteria. With help, they can use more complex criteria such as origin, behaviour and change. They use keys more confidently.	In retrospect, they recognis that of a number of method of sorting used in any particular case one may be more productive and usefu than the others.
Recognising patterns	When making observations, the children may seek patterns if prompted by the teacher. They can recognise the common factors in the information obtained by observing a number of instances. They are not able to describe the pattern formally. They may or may not be able to identify other instances which fit the pattern.	When making observations, the children look for patterns and recognise the more obvious patterns in their observations. With help, they describe the patterns orally. They will consider whether a new instance fits the pattern.	The children look for patterns, and with prompting are able to recognise patterns based on more complex observations. The process is assisted if the observations are made concurrently (or nearly so). Their oral description of the pattern improves and with prompting they consider whether new instances fit the pattern.	The children look more systematically for observations which form patterns, and become awar of the wider range of observations which may fo patterns. Most patterns wh they discern are in static properties, e.g. colour, shap form, etc. With help, they describe these patterns and consider whether new observations fit the pattern
Predicting	The children can make reasonable suggestions based on observations over a period of time. They can recognise some causal relationships.	The children make reasonable suggestions based on observations and when causal relationships are recognised they can, with help, make suggestions about effects that the cause will produce. They can suggest immediate and also future changes.	The children can base their suggestions on a number of observations viewed as a whole. They recognise a relationship but may not be able to give a clear oral description.	The suggestions which the children make are increasin consistent with all the observational evidence. Th children become aware tha the reliability of their suggestions about future events or changes depends the reliability of the observations on which the are based.
Controlling variables	The children start to identify one or two obvious variables. These may or may not be relevant. The children are able to find out whether or not they are relevant. When a relevant variable is identified, the children are able to find a way of controlling it if prompted by the teacher.	The children look for variables and notice more possibilities which may or may not be relevant. They can decide whether the more obvious are relevant and, with the help of the teacher, can find means of control.	The children look for variables and begin to draw on their experience in considering whether or not the variables are relevant. They are increasingly able to identify relevant variables and, with help, to find means of control.	The children are concerned look for variables. They recognise that there canno a fair test if the relevant variables are not controlled They can investigate two o three of the obvious ones a with help, control those fo to be relevant.
Investigating	The children can design and carry out simple investigations with minimal help with practicalities. They notice the more relevant variables and investigate them as part of their overall plan. With help, they suggest ways of controlling the variables and include this control in the design and execution of their investigations.	In designing their investigations, the children become increasingly aware of the possible wide range of variables. With help, they suggest means of identifying and controlling relevant variables and include this in the design and execution of their investigations. In discussion, they will agree that repetition is desirable and with prompting will repeat investigations.	Their range of investigations includes those of the type 'What happens when . . .?', 'What happens if . . .?' and 'Which is best?'. They start to consider investigation of suggestions based on recognised patterns.	They become better at formulating suggestions ar questions for investigation They are more aware of the possible range of variables and this awareness is increasingly reflected in the design and execution of the investigations.

	Year 3		Year 4	
	Level 1	**Level 2**	**Level 1**	**Level 2**
Classifying	The range of sorting criteria which the children can use independently and with confidence becomes wider, to include origin, behaviour and change. The children begin to consider in advance which sorting criteria will be most useful for a particular purpose, and with help they can make an appropriate suggestion. They are increasingly aware of the need to use keys, and with help they can construct them.		They make decisions about which sorting criteria to use with increasing independence, and the methods suggested are increasingly appropriate. In retrospect, the children are able to comment on the appropriateness of their choice. They use simple keys with confidence, and more complex keys with help. They are able to construct simple keys with little help and can attempt more complex keys.	The children can classify into sets and subsets using simple and complex criteria selected appropriately by themselves. They can use and construct simple keys.
Recognising patterns	The children use appropriate observations to seek patterns. They consider not only static properties but also dynamic ones, including, for example, behaviour and change, and they consider observations over a period of time. They recognise these patterns with help and can describe them orally. They can attempt to produce a written statement of simpler patterns and are increasingly able to decide whether new observations fit the pattern.	The children recognise patterns of various kinds and with help can describe them orally and in writing. They are increasingly able to use the patterns as the basis for suggestions about future happenings. They can look for patterns in derived data, particularly mathematical data, and with help can discern patterns in this data.	The children are able more readily to recognise patterns in simple data, and with help to recognise patterns in mathematical data presented in both graphical and tabular form. They are increasingly able to describe the patterns clearly, both orally and in writing. They are able to identify other instances which fit the pattern and to discuss their reasons.	When making observations, the children seek patterns in the information obtained. They recognise common factors in the information obtained by observing a number of instances. They are able to recognise other instances which fit the pattern.
Predicting	With help, the children increasingly make suggestions based on the recognition of an observational pattern. With help, the children can give a clearer oral description of the pattern and consequently, their suggestions become more consistent with the recognised pattern. They use not only observations and derived data but also known concepts.	The children base their suggestions on more complex patterns, including change and behaviour.	Increasingly, the children are able, with help, to make suggestions based on derived data. Their suggestions are more precise and take in all the evidence. They attempt to assess the likely reliability of their suggestions.	The children base their suggestions on firm evidence, including recognised patterns. There is increasing recognition of causal, as distinct from casual, relationships. They use known concepts in making their suggestions.
Controlling variables	The children attempt to identify variables and investigate two or three of the most obvious. With help, they control those that are found to be relevant. They start to consider in retrospect whether they have identified all the relevant variables and whether they have effectively controlled those that have been identified.	The children are increasingly able to identify variables and use their accumulating experience in eliminating non-relevant ones. They can find means of controlling simple variables and with help tackle more complex situations.	As for Year 3 Level 2. In retrospect, the children are increasingly concerned with whether relevant variables have been completely identified and whether they have been effectively controlled.	The children are aware of a wide range of variables and, on most occasions, can identify and control those which are relevant.
Investigating	With help, they start to investigate suggestions based on recognised patterns. They are increasingly concerned with the reliability of their investigations. They appreciate the need for repetition and when prompted repeat observations and measurements.	With help, they can investigate suggestions based on mathematical data. They can work with care and accuracy. They are aware of the need for repetition to check accuracy, and carry out checks without prompting.	The children can investigate simple suggestions and questions with minimal help. They design and carry out simple investigations, paying regard to obvious variables and their control. They consider the level of accuracy required and can use ideas about estimation and approximation.	The children can design and carry out simple investigations with confidence. They can identify and control most relevant variables. They can review their investigations critically and they check their results by repetition.

Extension B   Scientific ideas

These are the ideas to which we would like children to be exposed and
which we would like them to explore. As stated already, they will meet
these ideas in their own environment, and so will be able to experience
and explore them in a familiar setting. It is difficult to indicate briefly the
depth of understanding which it is hoped children will acquire, but as
ideas arise in the science activities the depth of treatment intended will
clearly explained. Indeed, in most cases, the activities themselves will the
the story.

It will soon become clear to teachers using the materials that it is
necessary to return to ideas time and time again, each time probing them
more searchingly and using the children's developing skills and abilities
to help them towards greater understanding. The role of language in the
process is crucial and this aspect is taken up in Extension D, Language
science.

Children's exposure to scientific ideas

The basic ideas are listed below and on page 114. Table 3 overleaf shows
at which point in the scheme in the infant years particular scientific ideas
are explored. The ideas are presented in a way that will enable children
working at a particular level to gain appropriate experience and
understanding. In Table 3, the numbering of the scientific ideas
corresponds to the numbering used for the statements in the following
list. The topic letters and activity reference numbers denote the specific
activities in which the ideas are introduced. A key to the topic letters
appears on page 114.

Basic ideas

1 Sets – the concept of a set as a group of items sharing a common
   feature.

2 Colour – primary, secondary, black, white, shades, etc.

3 Shape
   3.1 2D – square, rectangle, circle, ellipse, triangle.
   3.2 3D – cube, cuboid, sphere, ellipsoid, cylinder, triangular prism
   3.3 Symmetry – mirror images.

4 Concept of quantity

5 Measurement of quantity
   5.1 Direct comparison.
   5.2 Arbitrary units.
   5.3 Standard units.
   5.4 Approximation, estimation.

6 Spatial relationships and direction, e.g. under, behind, backwards,
   etc.

Ideas about the physical world

7 The world around us
   7.1 There is air round the earth.
   7.2 Air contains water vapour.
   7.3 Soil is a mixture of things which come from rocks as well as
        some material which was once living.
   7.4 The apparent movement of sun, moon and stars follows a
        regular predictable pattern.
   7.5 The seasons follow a regular pattern related to the position of
        the sun.
   7.6 Water flows to a common level.
   7.7 Floating and sinking depend on both the kind of material and
        on the shape.

8 Movement and energy

    8.1 The (average) speed of an object depends on the distance it travels in a certain time.

    8.2 Force is needed to move a stationary object or to alter the direction of travel of a moving object.

    8.3 Objects are pulled towards the earth; weight is a measure of how hard that pull is.

    8.4 The greater the force, the more energy is required.

    8.5 Energy can be supplied in many ways: by burning fuel, by eating food, or by doing work and storing the energy, e.g. in an elastic band, in a stretched spring, etc.

    8.6 The faster an object moves, the more energy it has.

    8.7 A moving object is stopped or slowed down by energy being removed from it.

    8.8 This energy may appear as heat (as in braking).

    8.9 An object moving on a surface must overcome friction.

9 Structure and forces

    9.1 Forces are needed to change the shape of an object.

    9.2 The strength of an object or structure depends on its shape and on the material from which it is made.

    9.3 For a given force, the pressure is greater the smaller the area on which it is exerted.

10 Magnets and electricity

    10.1 Magnets can attract or repel each other.

    10.2 Some materials are attracted by a magnet and some are not.

    10.3 Some materials can be magnetised and some cannot.

    10.4 Some materials conduct electricity and some do not.

    10.5 For an electric current to flow, there must be a complete circuit of conducting material.

11 Light and sound

    11.1 Light travels in straight lines.

    11.2 Objects can be seen because of the light they give out or reflect.

    11.3 Sound comes from vibrating objects.

12 Change

    12.1 Change may be reversible or irreversible.

    12.2 Change of state is reversible.

    12.3 Cooking usually produces irreversible changes.

    12.4 During a change of state, the substance itself does not alter, it merely changes its form.

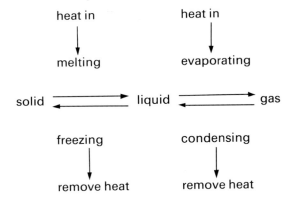

13 Properties of materials

    13.1 Different materials have different properties.

    13.2 Materials are used for purposes for which their properties make them appropriate (paper, wood, metals, plastics, wool, cotton, synthetic fibres, glass, brick, stone, rubber).

    13.3 Materials can be classified by consideration of their properties, e.g. metals, plastics.

    13.4 Some substances are soluble in water and some are not.

    13.5 Some substances do not dissolve in water but dissolve in other liquids, e.g. cooking oil. (continued on page 114)

Table 3   Children's exposure to scientific ideas

Basic ideas		Book A Level 1	Book A Level 2	Book B Level 1
Sets	1	$H^{1,2,7}$ $C^{2,3,7}$ $Cl^{1,7}$	S^6 $B^{2,3,4,5}$ Co^2 Ca^1 Sc^3	Sh^2 $Su^{1,7}$ P^4 Sw^1 K^4
Colour	2	$H^{1,6}$ Wh^4 $C^{1,2,5,6,7}$ Cl^1 $W^{2,4}$	$S^{1,2,3,4}$ $B^{2,3}$ Co^1 $Sc^{1,3,6}$	Sh^1 $P^{2,3}$ $Sw^{1,4}$ Pt^4 $K^{4,5}$
Shape	3.1	H^3 $Bo^{1,2}$ Wh^4 $C^{2,4}$ Cl^4 $W^{1,3}$	S^1 $B^{2,4,6}$ $Co^{5,6}$ $Sc^{4,7}$	P^2 $Pt^{1,2,3}$
	3.2	H^3 $Bo^{1,2}$ $C^{2,7}$ Cl^4 W^3 C^4	$S^{1,2}$ B^2 $Co^{5,6}$ Sc^4 $Co^{3,8}$	$Su^{1,5,7}$ $Pt^{1,2,3}$
	3.3	Cl^5		Sh^1 Pt^1
Concept of quantity	4	H^7 $Bo^{1,2,3}$ $Wh^{1,2,3}$ $C^{2,4,6}$ $Cl^{1,3,4,5,6}$ $W^{1,2,3}$	$S^{3,5,6}$ $B^{2,3}$ $Co^{2,6}$ Ca^1 $Sc^{2,3,6,7}$	$Su^{1,3,5}$ $P^{2,3,6}$ $Sw^{3,4}$ Pt^4 $K^{1,2,7}$
Measurement of quantity	5.1	H^7 $Bo^{1,2,3}$ $Wh^{1,2,3}$ $C^{2,4,6}$ $Cl^{1,3,5,6}$ $W^{1,2,3}$	$S^{3,5,6}$ B^2 $Co^{2,6}$ Ca^1 $Sc^{2,3,6,7}$	Sh^3 Su^1 $P^{2,3,6}$ Pt^4
	5.2		Co^4	Sh^1 Su^5 $Sw^{3,4}$ $K^{1,2,7}$
	5.3			
	5.4			
Spatial relationships	6	H^3 $Wh^{1,4}$ Cl^5	S^1 B^3 Sc^8	$P^{1,2,3}$
The world around us	7.1		Sc^4	
	7.2	W^4	B^6 Sc^5	
	7.3		S^6 Sc^3	
	7.4			
	7.5	W^1		
	7.6		Co^8 Sc^8	Su^3
	7.7	W^3	S^6 B^5 $Sc^{4,6}$	P^1 K^3
Movement and energy	8.1			
	8.2	$Wh^{1,2}$	Ca^1 Sc^7	
	8.3	H^3 Wh^2		
	8.4	$Wh^{1,2}$	Ca^4	
	8.5		S^2 Ca^1 Sc^7 Ca^4	
	8.6			
	8.7			
	8.8			
	8.9			
Structures and forces	9.1	C^2	Sc^4	Su^7
	9.2			Su^7
	9.3			Sh^4 P^1
Magnets and electricity	10.1			
	10.2			
	10.3			
	10.4			
	10.5			
Light and sound	11.1	W^1		Sw^1
	11.2			
	11.3	Bo^4 $C^{3,4}$	Co^7	$P^{4,5}$
Change	12.1	H^6 Bo^3 $W^{2,3,4}$	S^2 B^6 $Sc^{4,6}$	$Su^{4,5}$ Sw^4 $K^{1,3}$
	12.2		S^2 B^6 Sc^6	Su^4
	12.3	Bo^3 W^4		Su^5 K^1
	12.4	Bo^3 $W^{2,3,4}$	S^2 B^6 $Sc^{5,6}$	$Su^{2,3,4,5}$
Properties of materials	13.1	Bo^4 $C^{4,5}$ $Cl^{6,7,8}$ C^7	B^4 $Co^{1,2,3,4,5,6}$ $Ca^{1,2,3,4}$ $Sc^{1,3,4}$	Sh^4 Su^1 P^5 $K^{1,2,3,4,6,7}$
	13.2	$C^{4,7}$ $Cl^{6,7,8}$	B^4 Co^5 $Ca^{2,3,4}$ Sc^4 Co^6	Sh^4 $Su^{1,2,7}$ K^6
	13.3		B^5 $Co^{1,2,4,7}$	Su^1 P^5
	13.4			$Su^{2,6}$ Sw^2 $K^{2,3,4,5}$
	13.5			
	13.6		B^2 $Co^{3,8}$ $Sc^{1,6}$	Su^3 K^3
Weather	14.1			
	14.2			
	14.3			
	14.4	$W^{2,3}$		
Living/non-living	15.1	H^8 $Wh^{1,3,4}$ C^6	$S^{1,3,5}$ B^1	Sh^1
	15.2		S^3 B^1	
	15.3		S^3	
	15.4			
Food chains	16.1		S^2	$P^{1,3,6}$
	16.2		S^2	
	16.3	H^8	$S^{1,5}$	
	16.4	H^8	$S^{1,5}$	
	16.5			
Living together	17.1	$H^{1,2,3,4,5,6,7,8}$ $C^{3,6}$	$S^{1,2,3,5}$	$P^{1,2,3,6}$
	17.2			$P^{1,2,3,6}$
	17.3			$P^{2,3}$
	17.4			
Life cycles	18.1			
	18.2			
	18.3	H^8 C^6	S^5	
	18.4		$S^{1,5}$	
People	19.1	$Wh^{1,2,3,4}$	$B^{1,3}$	
	19.2	$Wh^{1,2,3}$	$B^{1,3}$	P^3
	19.3	$H^{1,2,3,4,5,6,7}$ $Bo^{3,4}$ $C^{1,2,3,4,5,6,7}$ $Cl^{1,2,6}$ W^4	$S^{1,2,3,6}$ $B^{2,4}$ $Co^{1,3,4,7}$	Sh^4 $Su^{2,3,4,5,6}$ P^5 Sw^2 Pt^4 $K^{4,5}$
	19.4	$Cl^{6,7,8}$		Sh^4
	19.5		B^3	
	19.6			
	19.7			

sic as		Book B Level 2	Book C Level 1	Book C Level 2
s	1	E^1 $Po^{1,2,4}$ Pa^5	N^1 G^4 Hn^5 Sg^3	T^4
our	2	$E^{1,2}$ F^1	$G^{2,5,6}$ $Ce^{2,3,4,5}$ G^1 N^5	A^2 $Fa^{1,4}$ Fm^2 We^3 A^3 Fa^5
pe	3.1	M^1 $Pa^{1,2}$	Hn^1 $Hs^{2,3}$ G^1	T^7
	3.2	$E^{2,5}$	Hn^1 $Sg^{2,4}$ G^4 Ce^1	$T^{1,2,3,6}$
	3.3	E^2 Po^3	G^6 Hs^3 $Sg^{2,6}$	A^3
ncept of ntity	4	$E^{1,4,6,7}$ $F^{2,3,4}$ Pa^3		
asurement uantity	5.1	E^1 Po^2 $Pa^{3,4,6}$	G^1 Hn^3 $Ce^{1,3}$ $N^{2,5}$	
	5.2	E^4 $F^{2,3,4,6}$ M^2 $Pa^{3,6}$	G^4 Ce^1 G^5 N^1	T^7 We^4
	5.3	$E^{6,7}$	G^3 $Hn^{1,3}$ $Ce^{1,4}$ Hs^1 $N^{1,2,3}$ $Sg^{1,2,3,4,5,6}$ $G^{1,2,4}$ Hs^2	$T^{1,5}$ $A^{2,3,5}$ $Fa^{2,3}$ $Fm^{2,4,5}$ $We^{2,3,5,6}$ A^1
	5.4		Sg^6	A^1 $Fm^{2,5}$ We^1
tial tionships	6	$E^{2,4}$ $F^{5,6}$ M^4 $Pa^{1,2,7}$	$Hs^{1,2,3}$ $Sg^{1,2,6}$ G^2	$T^{1,2,3,4,5}$ $We^{1,7}$
world und us	7.1	F^4	$G^{1,3}$ Hn^1 Sg^1 G^4 $Ce^{1,4}$	$We^{3,4,7}$ Fa^3 Fm^4
	7.2		G^1 $Ce^{1,4}$ Sg^1	
	7.3			
	7.4			We^1
	7.5			
	7.6	F^5		$T^{6,7}$ A^5 Fm^1
	7.7	E^2 F^5	Sg^2 Hn^3	$T^{3,7}$
vement and rgy	8.1	Po^1 $F^{2,3}$ Pa^3	Hs^1 Sg^5 G^3	$T^{1,2,3,4,5,6,7}$ We^7
	8.2	F^4 M^2 $Pa^{1,2,7}$	$G^{3,4}$ Hs^2 $N^{1,2}$ $Sg^{3,4}$ Hs^3	$T^{2,5}$ Fa^2
	8.3	E^2 $Pa^{2,4,7}$	Hs^1	$T^{2,3,5,7}$ Fa^1
	8.4	$Pa^{1,7}$	G^3	$T^{4,5}$ $Fm^{1,3}$ $T^{2,3,7}$ We^7
	8.5			$T^{4,5}$ Fm^1
	8.6			T^4
	8.7			T^4
	8.8	Pa^1		$T^{2,3,4}$ Fa^1
	8.9	Pa^1	N^4	$T^{5,6,7}$ Fa^2 $Fm^{3,5}$
uctures d forces	9.1	E^2	Hn^1 Ce^4 $Sg^{2,3}$	$Fa^{1,2}$ Fm^3
	9.2		Hn^3 $Hs^{1,4}$ $N^{1,2,3}$	
	9.3		Hn^3	
gnets and ctricity	10.1	Po^1	Hn^5	
	10.2	Po^1	Hn^5	
	10.3		Hn^5	
	10.4	Po^4		
	10.5	Po^4		
ht and und	11.1	M^4	Ce^5 Sg^6 Hn^4	$We^{1,2}$
	11.2		Hn^4	
	11.3	M^2	Hs^5	
ange	12.1	E^2 M^2 Pa^5	G^6 $Hn^{1,3}$ $Ce^{1,2,3,4}$ Sg^1 G^1	$T^{6,7}$ $A^{1,3,4}$ $Fa^{3,4,5}$ $Fm^{1,2,3,5}$ $We^{2,4,6,7}$
	12.2		Ce^2	Fa^3
	12.3	M^4	G^6	$Fm^{2,5}$
	12.4		G^1 $Ce^{2,4}$ Sg^1	A^1 $Cs^{3,4}$ Fa^5 Fm^2 $We^{3,4,5}$
operties of terials	13.1	$E^{2,4}$ $Po^{1,4}$ $M^{2,4}$ $Pa^{1,5}$	$Hn^{1,2,3,5}$ $Ce^{1,2,3,4}$ $Hs^{1,4}$ $N^{1,2,3,4}$ $Sg^{1,3,4}$	$T^{3,4,6}$ $Fa^{1,2,3,4}$ $Fm^{1,3}$ $We^{2,4}$ Fa^5
	13.2	Po^4 $M^{2,4}$ $Pa^{1,5}$	G^6 $Hn^{1,2,3}$ $Ce^{1,2,3,4}$ $Hs^{1,4}$ $N^{1,3,4}$ $Sg^{1,3,4}$	$T^{3,4,6}$ $Fa^{1,2,3,4}$ Fm^3 Fa^5
	13.3	$Po^{1,4}$ F^1 M^2 Pa^5	Hn^5 N^4	T^4 Cs^4
	13.4		Hn^3	A^1 Fm^5 We^4
	13.5			
	13.6	M^3	Ce^2	Fm^1
eather	14.1		Sg^1	$We^{1,2,4}$
	14.2			We^5
	14.3			We^7
	14.4			
ving/non ing	15.1	$E^{3,4,5,6,7}$	$G^{1,2,3}$ Hn^4 G^4	$A^{1,3,4,5,6}$ Fm^4 A^2
	15.2			
	15.3	F^1		
	15.4			$A^{1,2,3,4,5}$ Fm^4 A^6
od chains	16.1	F^4	Hn^4	
	16.2			$A^{2,4,5,6}$
	16.3	$E^{3,4,5,6,7}$	$G^{1,2,3}$	Fm^4
	16.4	$E^{3,4,5,6,7}$		Fm^4
	16.5			
iving together	17.1	$E^{1,3,4,5,6,7}$ F^1 M^4	$G^{1,2,3,4,5,6}$ Hn^4	$A^{1,2,3,4,5,6}Fm^4$
	17.2		$G^{3,4}$ Hn^4	$A^{1,2,3,4,5,6}$
	17.3	$E^{3,4,5,6,7}$	$G^{3,4,5}$ Hn^4 $G^{1,2}$	$A^{1,2,3,4,5,6}$ Fm^4
	17.4			$A^{2,3,4,5,6}$
ife cycles	18.1	$E^{3,4,5,6,7}$	$G^{3,4}$	$A^{1,3,5}$ Fm^4
	18.2	$E^{3,4,5,6,7}$	$G^{3,4}$	$A^{1,3,5}$ Fm^4
	18.3	$E^{3,4,5,6,7}$	$G^{3,4}$	$A^{1,3,5}$ Fm^4
	18.4	$E^{3,4,5,6,7}$	$G^{3,4}$	$A^{1,3,5}$ Fm^4
eople	19.1	$Po^{2,3}$ $F^{2,4}$ M^1		$A^{2,4}$
	19.2	$Po^{2,3}$ $F^{2,4}$ M^1		
	19.3	E^4 Po^1 $M^{1,4}$	$Hn^{3,4}$ $Hs^{4,5}$	Fm^2
	19.4			Fa^3
	19.5			
	19.6	F^4 M^1		
	19.7			

13.6 Substances can be classified as liquids, solids or gases according to their properties, e.g. water, cooking oil, washing up liquid; ice, wood, glass; steam, air.

14 Weather

14.1 The sun provides us with warmth.

14.2 Rain falls when there are clouds.

14.3 Clouds can stop the sun's rays (light and heat) from reaching

14.4 The type of weather we have is associated with the seasons.

Ideas about the living world

15 Living/non-living

15.1 Living things have common properties: growth, respiration, reproduction, nutrition, excretion, and possibly movement.

15.2 Non-living things do not have these properties.

15.3 Some non-living things were once alive.

15.4 Some non-living things occur naturally, e.g. rocks, and some are man-made.

16 Food chains

16.1 Living things must eat; they need water and air.

16.2 Big animals may eat little animals; eventually down the chain animals eat plants.

16.3 Plants need food and water.

16.4 Plants get their food from the soil.

16.5 The food which plants take from the soil must be replaced.

17 Living together

17.1 Plants and animals are very diverse in form.

17.2 Their form fits their environment: animals, fish, birds and plan

17.3 Plants and animals are sensitive to their environment and respond to it.

17.4 Plants and animals in a particular environment are dependent on each other.

18 Life cycles

18.1 All living things have a fixed life cycle.

18.2 The life cycle of all members of the same species is the same.

18.3 Parents produce offspring of the same kind as themselves.

18.4 The life cycles of living things are often linked to seasonal change.

19 People

19.1 People are living things. They exhibit variability.

19.2 They share the common properties of all living things.

19.3 They are able to explore the environment by using their sense

19.4 They are able to protect themselves from the environment.

19.5 Children must spend many years learning to care for themselves; this contrasts with other animals.

19.6 The different life processes take place in different defined part of the body.

19.7 Apart from the sex organs and those functions which are sexually controlled, the bodies of all people are the same and function in the same way.

Key to Table 3 on pages 112 and 113

Topics

Year 1: Harvest H, Bonfire night Bo, What can I do? Wh, Christmas C, Clothes Cl, Winter W, Spring S, The bathroom B, The cook Co, The caretaker Ca, School holidays Sc.

Year 2: The shoe shop Sh, The supermarket Su, Pets P, The sweet shop Sw, The post Pt, Jobs in the kitchen K, Easter E, The police Po, The firefighter F, Milk M, The park Pa.

Year 3: In the garden G, Hallowe'en Hn, Celebrations Ce, Jobs in the house Hs, The newsagent N, Spots and games Sg, Transport T, Animals A, Fabrics Fa, The farm Fm, Weather We.

Extension C   Summary of the experiences provided by the activities in Science through Infant Topics, Teachers' Books A, B and C

This summary identifies the main ideas which are explored in each activity in *Teachers' Books A, B* and *C*. As the scheme progresses, teachers will need to check the children's record sheets to see which activities individual children have carried out; of course, the extent to which children retain the ideas they have encountered will vary. Teachers should always be prepared to adjust the level of discussion as the children reveal their thinking through the comments they make and the ideas they express.

In Table 3, Extension B, page 112, the activities which contribute towards the development of children's understanding of particular concepts are identified.

Teachers' Book A: Level 1

Harvest
H1 Fruits are different colours. They can be sorted by colour. Certain colours are associated with particular ripe fruits.
H2 Fruits have different surface textures. They can be sorted by texture. Certain textures are associated with particular fruits.
H3 Fruits have different shapes. The shape of an object (e.g. a fruit) determines whether it will roll and how it will roll.
H4 Different fruits have different smells. Some fruits have a peel which may smell different from the fruit inside. Certain smells are associated with particular fruits.
H5 Some things taste sweet and some taste sour. For example, some varieties of apples taste sweet, and some sour. Oranges taste sweeter than lemons. Lemons taste sour.
H6 When an apple is cut and exposed to the air it turns brown. Different varieties of apples turn brown at different rates.
H7 Fruits contain pips, stones or seeds which vary in size, shape, colour, and texture.
H8 Pips, stones and seeds will germinate and grow if planted. Some germinate before others and some grow more quickly than others. The taste of bean sprouts changes as they grow.

Bonfire night
Bo1 Cylinders have curved and flat surfaces. The end of a cylinder forms a circle. A cylinder is the same width (diameter) at any point along its length. Several small cylinders of the same width (diameter) can be put together to form one longer cylinder.
Bo2 Cones have curved and flat surfaces. One end of a cone is wider than the other. A cone can be cut into a series of discs.
Bo3 When potatoes are cooked in their skins, changes take place. Margarine melts on hot potato. Potatoes cooked in their skins will cool at different rates if left with skins intact, skins removed or cut in half.
Bo4 Percussion instruments make different sounds. They can be used to make loud or soft sounds. Sounds can be made by tapping other objects. Some materials make louder noises than others.

What can I do?
Wh1 When we jump, both feet are in the air at once. Some children can jump higher than others, and some further. High or long jumps are harder work than low or short jumps.
Wh2 In equal volumes, some materials feel heavier than others when we lift and carry them. It is harder work carrying a heavy weight than a light weight. We can lift with different parts of our body, e.g. feet.

EXTENSION C

Wh3 We have the same number of fingers (plus thumbs) as toes. We c
achieve a wider range of movement with our fingers than with ou
toes. We can pick up things more easily with our fingers than witl
our toes. We can align thumb and index finger. Some animals do
not have fingers like ours and they may use their mouths to pick
things up.

Wh4 We have particular features on our faces. We can move parts of o
faces in various ways. The way we move and hold our faces can
show the way we feel.

Christmas

C1 Objects can be matched one to one by colour (e.g. fairy lights and
beads).

C2 The texture and shape of a balloon change when it is inflated
(rubber stretches; the 2D shape becomes a 3D shape).

C3 Nuts have various shapes, sizes, colours, and textures. All the nuts
one kind are different but they also have recognisable similarities. A
nut contains a kernel which can be seen when the shell is cracked
open.

C4 Bells of different types have some differences and some similarities
They are made from different metals but these metals have similar
properties.

C5 A fine powder (e.g. icing sugar) will pour like a liquid.

C6 Holly has leaves, stems and berries. The top surface of a leaf is
different from the underside. The leaves have sharp points which va
in number. The berries contain a seed which can be planted and wi
produce a holly tree.

C7 Objects (e.g. shiny Christmas tree baubles and glittered ping pong
balls) look shiny (reflect light) in different ways.

Clothes

Cl1 A collection of objects (e.g. buttons) can be sorted in a variety of
ways.

Cl2 Materials have different textures. The texture is identified by touch
alone. The material can be identified by touch.

Cl3 Objects (e.g. sets of clothes and dolls) can be ordered and matche
by size.

Cl4 The body has a particular shape. Clothes are made in shapes to
match the parts of the body they fit.

Cl5 Some pairs (e.g. gloves) are mirror images. Some pairs (e.g. socks
are identical. Our two feet and two hands are mirror image pairs.

Cl6 Different materials have different heat retaining properties. Gloves
are made from many different kinds of material. A glove will reduce
the heat loss from the object it covers (e.g. a small hot water bottle

Cl7 A collection of objects (e.g. hats) can be sorted by purpose.

Cl8 Some fabrics will allow water to run through them, and some will
soak up water. Others will not: these are termed 'waterproof'.

Winter

W1 If an object is held vertically and at right angles to the sunlight it m
cast a sharp shadow longer but not noticeably wider than itself.

W2 Fresh snow is cold, white and soft. When we walk on it, we leave
footprints. It melts on our hands. A full jar of snow taken indoors w
melt and the resulting water will not fill the jar.

W3 Ice is hard, cold and brittle. Pieces of ice always float in water, no
matter what size or shape the pieces are. Ice melts on our hands or
when warmed by being taken indoors.

W4 Bread changes in size, colour, texture and temperature when it is
toasted. We heat it to toast it. Moisture comes from the bread.
Margarine melts on the hot toast. Bread shrinks as it dries (it loses
moisture).

Teachers' Book A: Level 2

Spring

S1 A hyacinth has roots, bulb, stem, flower and leaves. The leaves have a particular shape, colour and texture pattern. The bulb has layers, and feels wet inside. The roots, leaves and stem arise from a particular part of the bulb.

S2 Solid lard does not move or change shape when tilted in a pan. When heated, the lard melts and will then move and change shape when the pan is tilted. When left to cool, the lard becomes solid again. Birds like to eat a variety of food including fruit, seeds, cake and lard.

S3 A living thing (e.g. a real flower) and a non-living thing (e.g. its artificial replica) have some differences and some similarities. The real flower eventually wilts and dies. It lasts longer in water. The artificial flower stays the same and water is not needed.

S4 The colour green can be seen in many living and non-living things. Many shades and tints are all considered green.

S5 Flower seeds can have many different sizes, shapes and colours. The seeds of one type of flower all have certain attributes in common. Different types of seeds can all be planted. They will germinate and grow at different rates and produce plants of their own kind.

S6 Potting compost is made up of an assortment of bits of different shapes and sizes. Some (sticks and leaf material) will float. Some (pebbles, grit, etc.) will sink.

The bathroom

B1 Living things (e.g. babies) have needs which non-living things (e.g. dolls) do not have. Water has certain properties which categorise it as a liquid (e.g. it will pour and splash). Water is clear and colourless. Steam rises from hot water but not from cold.

B2 Soap helps water to remove dirt. Soaps can have various sizes, shapes, colours and smells. Soap can be liquid or solid.

B3 We clean our teeth because food left on them can be harmful. Front teeth are a different shape from back teeth.

B4 Different types of fabric have some similarities and some differences. Some will absorb water better than others.

B5 Bath toys can be made from a variety of materials with different properties. Materials can be identified by their properties. Some toys sink and some float in water.

B6 The steam from hot water will condense as moisture on some surfaces. These then appear to be steamed up.

The cook

Co1 Sugar has various forms. It is made up of bits, which vary in size and colour depending on the type of sugar.

Co2 Spoons can be made from various materials. The material, shape and size are matched to the purpose of the spoon.

Co3 Fats can be liquid or solid and they differ in taste and appearance. They all repel water.

Co4 Sugar and salt can be distinguished by observing the size of the grains and other properties. Granulated sugar, salt and flour pour like liquids.

Co5 The properties of a cylinder make it a suitable shape for a rolling pin. The properties of wood make it a good material for a rolling pin.

Co6 The properties of a cone are utilised in a funnel.

Co7 In some cases, smell alone can be used to identify a substance (e.g. some items of food). Some items can be identified by the sound made when they are shaken in a container.

Co8 Utensils and vessels for food are shaped in particular ways because they are intended for use with solid or liquid food. The shapes relate to the properties of solids and liquids.

The caretaker

Ca1 The shape and structure of nails and screws determine how they are put into wood. The size and shape of the tools used must be appropriate.

Ca2 Some surfaces in buildings are shiny. Some are dull. Some material can be polished to make them shine. When metal is polished, the polishing rag becomes black.

Ca3 Some substances which are used in school will mark a Formica surface. Some of these substances are easier to remove than other.

Ca4 Scissors and knives are used for different types of cutting. Scissors will cut some things and not others. Some scissors cut better than others.

School holidays

Sc1 Sand behaves in some ways like a liquid, but a stone will not sink it; it does not find its own level; it will not soak into a tissue.

Sc2 Dry sand behaves differently from wet sand.

Sc3 Pebbles and stones can vary widely in size, colour, shape and texture. Water drains through pebbles, sand and soil at different ra

Sc4 Arm bands change shape (2D to 3D) when inflated. When deflate they can sink, and when inflated they float. Air is blown (pushed) into them to inflate them; it escapes as bubbles if released under water. Other objects, e.g. bottles, will float when they contain air.

Sc5 Water dries from the hands into the air. If a wet paper towel is exposed to the air and another is kept in an airtight container, the former will dry while the latter will remain wet.

Sc6 Both water and orange concentrate are liquids and can be seen to have the properties of liquids. When they are cooled in a freezer, they change to solids. When brought into a warm room, they change back to liquids.

Sc7 Wheels are circular. The larger the circle, the greater the distance travelled in one revolution.

Sc8 A ball will roll down a slope; water will run down a slope; the surface of water in a container remains level when the container is tilted. All these observations can be used to test whether an objec level or sloping.

Teachers' Book B: Level 1

The shoe shop

Sh1 Some pairs (e.g. shoes) are mirror images. Foot size varies from or person to another. Foot size may be related to height.

Sh2 Sets can be used to determine the order of popularity (e.g. of shoe fastenings).

Sh3 We walk on certain parts of our feet. Footprints made using talcum powder show this. Walking and tiptoe prints look different. Our shoes must be of appropriate size.

Sh4 Shoe uppers and soles can be made from various materials. The materials used and the structure of the shoe are suited to the purpose of the shoe.

The supermarket

Su1 Containers (e.g. in supermarkets) have various 3D shapes. They c be made from various materials, e.g. metal, glass or plastic, each o which has particular useful properties. A matrix can be used to sor collection of containers.

Su2 Peas are preserved in many different ways, and the processes change the way they look and feel. Water will boil if heated; we ca tell when it is boiling by observing its behaviour. The peas change when cooked and have different colours, tastes and textures. Whe frozen peas are added to boiling water, the water stops boiling an takes time to boil again.

Su3 The surface of a liquid is flat when settled. The liquid can move an change shape. Drips of a liquid will join the main body of the liqui and cannot be separated again. Different liquids flow at different speeds.

Su4 When solid chocolate is heated, it changes to liquid chocolate. Margarine and wax behave similarly. All three change back from liquid to solid when cooled. The solid wax and chocolate retain th shape of the container in which they cooled. Cooking oil will solidify if cooled sufficiently (refrigerated).

Su5 A hen's egg has a shell with a particular curved shape which determines the ways it rolls. The shell is solid. It can break. The yolk and white are liquid. The white is colourless. The yolk is contained in a skin which can be broken. If an egg in its shell is boiled in water, it changes in colour and from liquid to solid. This change is irreversible.

Su6 Sugar behaves in some ways like a liquid. It is made up of many small solid pieces. When added to water and stirred, it apparently disappears. The taste of the water is changed. The sugar has dissolved. Several types of sugar and salt dissolve in water.

Pets

P1 When water is poured (e.g. on to gravel in a fish tank), it exerts a force. The force can be spread in various ways (e.g. by using a saucer). Water weed is intended to grow in water. It changes in appearance when it is transferred from air to water.

P2 Goldfish have particular features on their bodies. Fins can be moved in particular ways; scales overlap in a particular direction suited to the flow of water past them as the fish moves.

P3 Budgerigars have particular features on their bodies. Feathers are of various sizes and overlap in a particular direction. Budgerigars move in particular ways. They seem to hear, although ears cannot be seen. A budgerigar's behaviour when offered a selection of foods can be observed.

P4 Budgerigar toys illustrate different kinds of motion – swinging, rocking, rolling. Objects can be sorted according to how they move.

P5 Different materials make different sounds when tapped. The surfaces on which they are placed can affect the sounds produced. Materials may be identified by the sound they make. Sounds can differ in pitch.

P6 The body of a small animal (mammal) has particular features. It has certain similarities to and differences from the goldfish and the budgerigar. We can investigate the animal's behaviour in various circumstances.

The sweet shop

Sw1 Sweets and sweet papers can be many different colours and different shades of one colour. Some sweets and sweet papers are translucent: light can be shone through the coloured sweet or sweet paper on to white paper to give a patch of that colour. Light can be shone through a coloured sweet paper on to an object thus apparently changing its colour.

Sw2 Sweets have various flavours. The sweets change as they are sucked. A boiled sweet will become soft and sticky in hot water. Strands of the sweet will harden quickly when cooled.

Sw3 Sweets of different types have different weights. The same weight of sweets will contain fewer heavy sweets than light sweets.

Sw4 When cooking, ingredients may need to be weighed. Ground almonds contain oil. An investigation can be set up to find out whether colour affects taste (e.g. different colours of marzipan).

The post

Pt1 Regular 3D shapes have a number of curved and flat surfaces. Some faces are identical. A regular 3D shape may be opened out flat to form a net composed of regular 2D shapes.

Pt2 Regular 3D shapes will pass through spaces of different shapes and sizes depending on which way round they are presented.

Pt3 Some regular 3D shapes will fit together without leaving spaces, while others will not. The same applies to 2D shapes.

Pt4 Size is not necessarily related to weight. Some large objects are lighter than smaller ones.

Jobs in the kitchen

K1 In cooking, ingredients may need to be weighed. Scone mixture must be heated to cook it. It changes in appearance and texture when

cooked. The addition of baking powder makes the mixture rise durin
cooking and alters the texture of the scone produced.

K2 Baking powder, sugar and salt have some features in common and
some differences. When added to water, baking powder produces
bubbles, while the others do not. Warm water speeds up the reactior

K3 Cold and hot water have different effects on greasy plates. Solid
margarine melts and floats when hot water is added; washing up
liquid, solid soap and washing powder each change the margarine
differently when added to the mixture. We can investigate which
cleanser is most convenient.

K4 Many shades and tints are classed as red. Some red substances have
a smell, others do not. Some will mark fabric. The cause of the mark
may be identified by colour and smell. Some marks wash out of fabri
more easily than others.

K5 Water will boil when heated. We can tell when it is boiling by
observing its behaviour. A tea bag may have little holes in it. Inside
are small pieces of various shapes and shades of brown. Boiling wate
changes colour when poured over the tea bag or on to loose tea. The
tea leaves change in appearance, texture and temperature. Somethin
from the tea leaves dissolves but the rest of the tea leaf does not
dissolve. 'Instant' tea may be the part of the tea leaf which dissolves.

K6 We use a variety of materials to cover walls. In a kitchen, the material
used may be required to resist a variety of stains. Some types of
surface are easier to clean without damage than others. We can
investigate which surfaces are satisfactory.

K7 Some paper towels are thicker than others, some contain more layers
and some are more absorbent. We can find out by investigation
which absorbs water best.

Teachers' Book B: Level 2

Easter

E1 Many flowers are yellow in colour. The flowers of one type have
particular features in common. Surrounding temperature affects the
rate at which cut flowers in tight bud, given water, open and
eventually die.

E2 When paste powder is added to water, the mixture thickens. When
inflated, balloons change in certain ways and remain the same in
other respects. Newspaper changes when soaked with paste, and
changes again as it dries out. The reflection of a hemisphere placed
on a mirror will make it appear to be a complete sphere.

E3 Seed potatoes may have shoots and roots growing from them. If
placed in damp soil, they will grow into potato plants.

E4 Seed peas given water on a paper towel will grow roots and shoots.
The shoots grow upwards and the roots grow downwards.

E5 Tomatoes and peppers contain seeds. The fresh seeds are different in
some ways from the seeds bought in packets. Fresh and packet seeds
may be planted and their progress compared.

E6 When sweet corn seeds are planted, the surrounding temperature will
affect their rate of germination and growth.

E7 When cucumber seeds are planted, the amount of light will affect the
growth of the young plants.

Police

Po1 Objects may be identified by describing their properties and
attributes.

Po2 People have unique features. They may be identified by describing
details of their appearance.

Po3 A reflection of one hand or foot in a mirror looks like the other hand
or foot. Hands have a palm and a back which differ in some respects.
Fingerprints can be made using an ink pad. Each child's fingerprints
are different from the other children's in some details.

Po4 Torches can be taken apart. They have a battery, switch and bulb.
The batteries must be placed in a particular direction to make the

bulb light when the switch is on. A bulb will only light when certain materials are placed across a gap in the circuit connecting it to a battery.

The firefighter

F1 New wood from trees has bark; the type of tree it comes from determines the characteristics of the bark. The wood inside has patterns in it. It can be flexible and it is damp. Burning changes the colour and texture of the wood. Burnt wood is not flexible. It will mark other objects.

F2 Children can move along the ground in many ways. Some ways are faster than others: the speed can be compared by racing. The competitors must all start and finish at the same places, and they must all start at the same time. Speed can also be compared by timing over a set distance. The less time taken, the faster the speed.

F3 The fasteners on clothes can affect the time it takes to get dressed. By comparing times taken, we can check whether practice improves performance.

F4 When we blow, air comes out. It is invisible but we can feel it. It moves things, and it forms bubbles under water. We breathe air in and out of our chests through our noses or mouths. Our chests change size as we breathe. We can measure how much air we breathe out by catching the air in a jar under water.

F5 The conditions for using a siphon to transfer water from one place to another are explored. The siphon tube, which can go up and down, must be full of water. The flow of water depends on the relative positions of the upper reservoir and the lower end of the siphon tube.

F6 We can find out which is the shortest route between two points by measuring length. We can find out which is the quickest route by measuring time taken.

Milk

M1 A milk straw is a cylinder. We can suck and blow air through it. If one end is covered, it prevents this. If one end of a straw full of milk is covered, the milk will not run out.

M2 Milk can be bought in different shaped bottles. Bottles that look very different may hold the same amount of milk. Some bottle tops need a bottle opener to remove them. The bottle opener uses a combination of pressing down and pulling up. Sterilised milk stays fresh longer than pasteurised milk. Pasteurised milk will stay fresh longer at a cooler temperature.

M3 Milk is a liquid. It can be heated and it will boil. If vinegar is added to hot milk, solid pieces form in the liquid. These curds can be separated from the liquid (whey) by various methods. If bread is soaked in milk and put in a warm place, moulds will form. Moulds will also grow on some cheeses.

M4 Milk bottles are transparent. We can see other objects through them. The appearance of the object changes very little when seen through the bottle. Water is transparent. We can see objects through it. The appearance of an object changes in various ways when seen through a bottle full of water.

The park

Pa1 We climb up the steps of a park slide and slide down the smooth ramp. It requires more effort (energy) to go up than down. Our feet will slide differently on a surface depending on the soles of our footwear. A surface can be made more or less slippery by putting other substances on to it, e.g. oil or chalk.

Pa2 A roundabout is circular. It rotates horizontally and its centre remains in the same place. Some circular objects can be rolled. They rotate vertically and the centre moves along, staying the same distance from the ground.

Pa3 A bead suspended on a short string will swing backwards and forwards at a faster rate than a bead suspended on a longer string. 'Pushing' it harder does not affect this.

Pa4 A pretend see-saw can be made to balance by adjusting the objects placed on either end.

Pa5 Cups and plates can be made from various materials including metal, plastic, pottery and paper. Picnic items need to have certain characteristics, e.g. they need to be unbreakable and light in weight and so they are made from materials which have these properties. Items made from metal, plastic and pottery can be immersed in water for washing without damage. Paper changes in water and paper items cannot be washed and used again.

Pa6 If an object is placed on a horizontal mirror, its reflection appears to be upside down. Reflections can be seen in various shiny surfaces. The shape of the surface affects the reflection. A wet, painted paper can be folded and opened to make a pattern so that one half resembles the reflection of the other.

Pa7 Water can leave a tap at different rates. The force of the water feels very different when the tap is full on compared with when the water only drips from the tap. A squeezy bottle can be used to make water move in drips and jets. The more force that is applied to the bottle, the more force the water has.

Teachers' Book C: Level 1

In the garden

G1 Many vegetables are the roots of plants and they have certain features in common. If a wet paper towel is left exposed to the air it will dry; the water goes into the air. The same happens with a slice of root vegetable. As it dries, it loses weight and shrinks in size. If a root vegetable is placed with its base in coloured water, the colour will travel through the root to its top.

G2 Fresh celery is rigid and will snap. It contains moisture. Celery deprived of water will become limp. If various parts of the celery are immersed in coloured water, only the celery with its base in water will show the colour rising up the stem to the leaves. A stem of celery which has been split, so that one part can be placed in water of one colour and the other part in another colour, will show one colour reaching certain leaf parts and the other colour reaching other parts.

G3 Dandelion seeds all share the same features. They can be planted and they will grow into dandelion plants. They fall through the air more slowly than some other seeds. They will travel in a draught and their particular formation helps them to do this. This is the way in which new plants grow where there were none before.

G4 Some trees have seeds. The seeds from one type of tree share the same features. Some types of tree seed fall more slowly than others. A test can be carried out to show this. The rate of fall seems to be related to the shape rather than the weight of the seeds.

G5 Blackberries change in colour and texture as they ripen. The colour from ripe blackberries will stain skin. If left, mould will grow on the ripe fruit. Investigations can be set up to find out which factors affect the rate at which mould grows on the fruit. Other ripe fruits behave in a similar manner.

G6 The leaf patterns inside a red cabbage can be observed when the cabbage is cut open in various directions. When cold water is added to some red cabbage and hot water is added to other red cabbage, the hot water changes colour more than the cold. When red cabbage is boiled in water with a piece of white cotton, the white cotton changes colour. The colour can be changed again by adding vinegar. The colour of the cloth will fade quickly if the cloth is left in the sun.

Hallowe'en

Hn1 A balloon is made of rubber. It can be stretched in various ways and will resume its original size when released. Air is used to stretch the balloon when it is blown up. It will only stretch so far, and then the rubber splits. An inflated balloon has a curved 3D shape which can be measured in various ways. We can set up an investigation to compare the force with which different pumps blow out air.

Hn2 Different types of paper absorb water paint differently. Paper can be treated with other substances, e.g. oil, fat or wax, to reduce its absorbency.

Hn3 The consistency of water changes when cellulose paste is added. Newspaper can be added to the mixture and it will absorb water. The resulting mixture is a type of papier mâché which can be used for models. As it dries, it loses weight and becomes hard. We can set up an investigation to compare this with papier mâché made with other white powders, e.g. salt, sugar or flour, instead of cellulose paste powder.

Hn4 We can observe the behaviour of small animals and record this over a period of time. We can put them in an environment offering light and dark areas and check at intervals how many animals are in each. Some small animals seem to prefer dark areas.

Hn5 A magnet will attract some objects and not others. All the objects it attracts are metal, but it does not attract all metal objects. If a paper clip is touching the magnet, the paper clip will attract another paper clip. The magnet will attract a paper clip through a sheet of paper. We can investigate the strength of different magnets by using this information.

Celebrations

Ce1 A piece of clay can be modelled. If all the clay is used, the shape can be changed while the weight remains the same. Clay loses weight and becomes harder as it dries. We can set up an investigation to discover which factors affect the rate at which clay dries.

Ce2 Candles are made of wax. The flame of a candle has certain features and behaves in certain ways. Wax melts and becomes liquid when heated. As it cools, it becomes solid again. It will melt and solidify repeatedly if heated and cooled. Wax can be various colours. Two colours of liquid wax can be mixed to form a new colour.

Ce3 Candles can be made by pouring liquid wax around a wick and cooling it to make the wax solidify. We can set up an investigation to discover whether the size, shape, or colour of a candle affects the size, shape or colour of the flame.

Ce4 We can set up investigations to compare the properties of the modelling materials clay, plasticine, and flour and salt dough. Plasticine becomes softer when warmed, while clay and dough dry out, losing weight and becoming hard. Water left on a saucer will eventually evaporate, while oil on a saucer will not.

Ce5 The colour of light produced by a torch can be changed by shining it through different colours of cellophane. If two differently coloured lights are shone on a white screen and overlap, the colour produced may not be the same as that produced if the two colours were mixed in paint.

Jobs in the house

Hs1 Bottles and tins have lids which open in various ways. Some can be opened by hand; others need a tool. If a screwdriver is used as a lever, the force is applied to the lever in one direction and the lever forces the object in the opposite direction. Using a lever of similar type, less effort is required to lift a weight if pressure is applied to the longer arm of the lever with the weight on the shorter arm than vice versa.

A balance with one arm longer than the other will require less weight on the longer than the shorter arm for the two to be equal.

Hs2 When two objects are suspended from a beam, as in a mobile, the beam will balance at a point nearer the heavier object than the lighter object. The distance of the hanging objects from the beam does not affect this.

Hs3 Ellipses can be drawn by holding a pencil in a loop of string around two fixed nails. The nearer together the nails are fixed, the 'fatter' the ellipse. The centre of gravity of a 2D card shape can be found. If the card is suspended at this point it will hang flat.

Hs4 The material used for a pinboard needs to be fairly soft. We can investigate the suitability of various samples of board and wall covering for this.

Hs5 Many different sounds may be heard around the house. An investigation can be set up to discover whether adults or children are better at identifying household sounds.

The newsagent

N1 Strings, cords and ropes can be of various thicknesses and made up in various ways. An investigation can be set up to compare the different breaking strengths of thin strings.

N2 Paper can be of various thicknesses, texture and colours. The variou papers behave differently when creased or wet. Investigations can b set up to discover which papers tear more easily than others.

N3 Some papers are stiffer than others. A test can be arranged to compare the relative stiffness of a range of papers.

N4 An investigation can be set up to compare the efficiency of various rubber erasers when used on different types of paper marked with a range of pens and pencils.

N5 An ink colour may be made up of several colours. Chromatography can be used to separate the various colours.

Sports and games

Sg1 A nylon swimming costume holds less water than a similar cotton costume. The amount of water held is equivalent to the difference i weight of the dry and wet costume. Investigations can be set up to find out which dries more quickly, and which conditions affect the rate of drying.

Sg2 Various types of float can be used as aids to swimming. They each support different weights before sinking. They can be made to support different weights by presenting them to the water at differing angles.

Sg3 Balls are made in different sizes and weights. The size and weight can be measured. The largest is not necessarily the heaviest. The smallest is not necessarily the lightest. The impacts of balls when dropped on to wet sand can be compared by measuring the depth of the holes they make. An investigation can be set up to find whic type of ball hits the sand hardest when dropped from a fixed heigh

Sg4 Investigations can be set up to discover which of a collection of balls is the best bouncer.

Sg5 A test can be arranged to find out how good each child is at aiming a ball so that it will roll along the ground and hit a skittle. Various methods of improving aim can then be investigated.

Sg6 If a ball is rolled to bounce off a wall into a receptacle, and the rolling point and receptacle are equidistant from the wall, the ball should hit the wall at a point half way between the receptacle and the rolling point. The distance of the receptacle and rolling point from the wall can be varied, as long as they remain equal. The bean of a torch can be shone along the same path to be reflected by a mirror, so that it shines on the receptacle.

Teachers' Book C: Level 2

Transport

T1 Regular 3D shapes have particular numbers of curved and flat faces. The shapes affect the way in which they roll. Narrow cylinders can b rolled to follow curves by tilting the track. Wide cylinders cannot be steered in the same way. The wheels on vehicles are usually narrow cylinders.

T2 To move a scooter, one foot pushes against the ground and the othe against the scooter. To move a pram or trolley, the feet push against the ground and the hands push against the pram or trolley. A loaded pram is harder to push. A load is easier to move by pushing on a pram or trolley than carrying by hand.

T3 To move a tricycle, the feet push against the pedals. In a fixed wheel tricycle, the pedals turn the front wheel which pushes against the ground. The other wheels roll along behind. In a chain tricycle, the pedals move the chain which turns the back wheels and then push against the ground. By turning one card wheel on a board, other wheels can be turned in various ways by linking them to the first wheel with a rubber band.

T4 A moving scooter can be stopped by pressing one foot against the ground. The more the foot grips the ground, the quicker the scooter stops. A brake block works by pressing against the wheel to stop it turning. Some materials used on a brake block grip more effectively than others and stop the wheel more quickly. The wheel becomes warm where the brake block presses.

T5 Given the same push, some toy lorries will travel further than others. Given the same push, a lorry will go further on the flat than uphill, and furthest downhill. Ramps and a device to give a 'standard push' can be made to investigate this.

T6 Some flat objects float. Some flat objects that sink can be made to float by changing their shape. Boats need to float and carry a cargo. An investigation can be set up to find the best shape for a toy boat so that it floats when empty and also when carrying a large cargo.

T7 More effort is required to move the hand through water palm first than edge on. Boats made from the same weight of plasticine will move differently through the water depending on their shape. The same is true of card boats.

Animals
A1 Sea water contains salt; fresh water, as found in ponds, does not. Frog spawn is found in fresh water. It follows a particular sequence of development through a tadpole stage to the adult frog. At each stage, behaviour can be observed and related to body features. Some body features are related to environment. The adult frogs will go on to produce more frog spawn.

A2 Spiders are found on land in many different habitats. They can be a variety of shapes, sizes and colours, but they all have particular features in common. Spiders produce a thread which they use to construct a web. The webs have a particular pattern, and trap food for the spiders.

A3 Caterpillars hatch out of eggs. They may need a specific type of food. They grow and can cast their skin. They all have particular body features in common. They follow a particular sequence of development though a pupa stage to adult moth or butterfly. The wings of the adult are mirror images of each other. The adult goes on to lay eggs and the sequence is repeated.

A4 Some ants live in soil. Many ants are found together in one place. They can move very quickly. In cool temperatures, the ants move more slowly. All ants have particular body features in common. We can observe their behaviour when presented with a variety of foods.

A5 Water snails can be found in ponds. They all have particular body features in common. They move in a particular way. From time to time, they open a tube on the surface of the water and appear to take in air. Snails may float or sink depending on how much air they are holding.

A6 Some animals live in a particular type of habitat. Others can live in a wide variety of habitats. This may be related to their food supply. Some animals have body features related to their environment. Animals of one type all have specific features in common by which they can be identified.

Fabrics
Fa1 Clothes wear out. The fabric may wear in particular places where rubbing occurs. An investigation can be set up to compare how quickly different types of fabric wear out when rubbed.

Fa2 Some fabrics tear more easily than others. A piece of fabric will tear in a particular direction, in relation to the weave. An investigation can be set up to compare the 'tearability' of different fabrics.

Fa3 Clothes may be worn to keep people warm. Some fabrics do this better than others. An investigation can be set up to compare how well different fabrics keep heat in.

Fa4 Dyes can be used to change the colour of fabrics. Different fabrics respond to dyes. Some fabrics will dye a deeper shade than others when treated similarly. Cotton and nylon can be distinguished by observing the results of dyeing.

Fa5 Water-based dyes will only be effective on fabric which absorbs water. Fabric treated with various waterproofing materials will not dye effectively. A pattern can be produced by treating certain parts of a piece of fabric in this way and then dyeing the fabric. Only the untreated parts will change colour.

The farm

Fm1 A layer of cream forms at the top of milk in a bottle. The cream can be removed; it is thicker than the remaining milk. The cream will turn to butter when shaken, but the skimmed milk will not.

Fm2 Rice and barley absorb some of the boiling water as they are cooked. They increase in volume and weight and change in texture. The changes in weight and volume can be measured. The number of grains of rice or barley does not increase.

Fm3 Flour is made by grinding wheat seeds to a powder. Grinding is best accomplished by rubbing between two hard surfaces.

Fm4 The food contained in the wheat seeds is intended for the young plant which could grow from the seed. This is also true of barley. The number of seeds produced on a plant grown from one wheat or barley seed can be investigated. The seed contains enough food for the young plant to start growing, but to continue it needs soil to provide food.

Fm5 Bread can be made using flour in various ways. When yeast is added, the dough will rise. Only dough containing yeast rises in this way. The yeast appears to produce bubbles in the dough. The volume of a loaf can be measured. Bread made with yeast is very different in volume and texture from bread made without yeast. How much the bread rises depends on the amount of yeast added.

Weather

We1 The shadow of an object falls on the side of the object which is opposite to the sun. During the day, the relative positions of the sun and a stationary object change, and the shadow position changes correspondingly. The height of the sun above the horizon affects the length of shadow. At the same time on different days, the shadow will fall in the same place. It is possible to make a shadow clock.

We2 Investigations can be set up to discover the conditions needed for fading to occur.

We3 Water left exposed to the air will evaporate. Investigations can be set up to discover the conditions which aid evaporation.

We4 Some substances dissolve in water. When the water they are added to evaporates, the substance is left behind. Investigations can be set up to discover the effect on the rate of evaporation of adding soluble substances to the water.

We5 The amount of rainfall each day can be measured and a record kept. The record will show that the amount can differ from one day to another. The apparatus used to collect and measure rain must be constructed in a particular way. This is a rain gauge.

We6 Temperature can be measured using a thermometer. At any one time, temperatures may be different in different places. At different times, the temperature may vary in the same place. A record can be kept to show changes in temperature.

We7 Wind direction and speed can be observed in various ways. A daily record can be kept to show changes. When a combined record showing rainfall, temperature, wind speed and direction, and general conditions is kept, patterns in the weather may begin to emerge.

Extension D   Language in science

The relationship between science and language for young children is twofold. Firstly, the rich variety of experiences which science offers requires a wide range of language to describe it, to comment on it and to report it. Secondly, if the observations and information acquired are to be understood, language is the means by which teachers and pupils can explore their common experience and extract from it their individual understanding.

In the early activities in *Longman Scienceworld*, we rely almost completely on spoken language. Most of the children will not yet have come to grips with the intricacies of the written word, so that teachers will be seeking ways of encouraging children to talk about what they are doing and what they are observing. Much of the talk will be among themselves (or even to themselves). A lot of the talk will involve the teacher who can take the opportunity to help the children to develop their language usage in different ways.

Using language to understand science is very much concerned with spoken language, even after children have a firm grasp of reading and writing. The spoken word is much closer to our thinking than the other language modes. It allows for the expression of the doubts and uncertainties which the various observations and puzzles of scientific activity present. We can um and ah and change our minds and say, 'Do you mean this or is this what you really mean?' We can listen to statements reflecting increasing understanding, and again question these. Everyone must make sense of an experience in his or her way. The interpretation of a new experience depends on the previous experiences which a person brings with him or her. One of the tasks of the teacher in introducing science is to help children explore the new experiences and relate these to themselves. An open-minded approach will help teachers quickly to become aware that there are no subject barriers in children's minds. Experiences from a wide variety of sources will often be brought together in interpreting these new experiences of science. This linking enables children to make sense of their new science experiences.

As the children's language skills develop and they begin to read and write, science activities provide a wide range of contexts for different kinds of writing, ranging from the descriptive to reporting sequential events. Suggestions have been made for this within the Science activities themselves and sometimes in the Further activities.

For the third infant year, it was decided that books for the children to read would be more appropriate than another *Starter Book* for teachers. One of the most important aspects of learning to read is wanting to read and going on wanting to read. Children of this age might not be able to tackle the reading of practical instructions, so these have been confined to the teacher's books. (Material which the children could read could be produced, but the children would still be teacher dependent for setting up activities, and this might simply make their reading frustrating.)

There are many simple science and technology related books available for young readers and many of them can be used as background material. They should be viewed with caution, however, if they are attempting to present scientific 'facts'.

Books about people and their jobs and occupations are likely to provide related reading of interest to children. The Ladybird series *People who help us* is a good example of this.

Longman Scienceworld does not have a sex bias and girls and boys should be able to relate to it equally well; however, teachers will have to look carefully at items such as reading books in the classroom if that lack of bias is to be preserved. The proportion of information books which are sex-stereotyped is still high, unfortunately.

Each child must arrive at his or her own understanding, and language is an important means by which understanding is derived from experience. Every opportunity for children to express their thinking and interact orally with each other should be seized upon. Science activities provide a rich source of such opportunities.

Extension E Using mathematics in science

Teaching mathematical concepts is not a direct objective of this science scheme but many opportunities do arise to use mathematical skills in a purposeful way. In particular, the concepts and skills associated with shape, length, weight and capacity are important in science as they are mathematics and these have been included as appropriate. For quantiti and shape, detailed suggestions are given throughout the scheme for their practical inclusion. The same consideration has been given to number work, but specific reference to this has not been made since teachers will recognise many instances where the practical situation provides excellent opportunities to reinforce the work being done in mathematics. Care has been taken to ensure that the work suggested closely matches the developmental stages normally covered in infant work. The details of these stages related to the science levels are showr in Table 2 on page 104.

The work is specifically tied in with the stages suggested in the *Nuffield Maths 5–11* scheme, and for teachers using this scheme Table shows the links. By no means are all the skills and concepts covered in these *Nuffield Maths 5–11* chapters practised, but where mathematics work is included it does not exceed the demands of these chapters. Whatever mathematics scheme is being used, teachers will wish to respond to the needs of particular children; for most children the activit suggested are at the appropriate level, and will provide a purposeful enrichment of their normal mathematics programme.

Table 4

Science through infant topics		Nuffield Maths 5–11 Quantities and shape							
Year 1	Level 1	L1:1 L1:2 S1:1 S1:2 S1:3 W1:1 W1:2 T1:1 T1:2 C1:1							*Teachers Handbo*
	Level 2	L1:3 L1:4 C1:2 C1:3 C1:4							
Year 2	Level 1	L1:5 L1:6 W1:3 W1:4 T1:3 T1:4 C1:5							
	Level 2	S2:1 S2:2 S2:3 S2:4 T2:1 T2:2 T2:3							*Teachers Handbo*
Year 3	Level 1	L2:1 L2:2 S2:5 W2:1 W2:2							
	Level 2	L2:3 L2:4 L2:5 W2:3 T2:4 T2:5 T2:6 C2:1 C2:2 C2:3 C2:4							

The numbering in this table is the same as is used in the Contents page in the *Nuffield Maths 5–11 Teachers' Handbooks*.

Extension F The development of technological ability and understanding (Making and doing)

A lot has been written about technology and what it is. For many non-specialist teachers, the picture which emerges is a daunting one; how can they translate the grand ideas into action? *Longman Scienceworld* tries to demystify technology and suggest activities which will enable children to acquire some technological skills. The children should have opportunities to investigate in situations where they really do need the information which the scientific investigation can produce.

Firstly, what do we mean by technology, and more importantly what do we mean by technology in the Making and doing activities suggested? Technology is a way of thinking which is useful in solving problems of a particular kind. Generally, these problems are expressions of some particular need. In real life, these problems may be very complex and complicated. In the classroom, where our concern is with how to set about solving the problems, our examples are simpler. For example, one of the first problems is 'Can you make a bag to carry fruit home from the fruit shop?' Another feature of technological problems which this illustrates is that they do not have right and wrong answers: some solutions are just better and some are worse. Often, one solution will be better in some ways than another and worse in other ways, and there has to be a balancing of desirables and undesirables. There is a strong element of optimisation.

Another salient feature of technological problem solving is that we have to think about the problem from all sorts of points of view. For example, in making a bag, we have to think first of all about what the bag must do – what properties it should have. It will have to carry a fairly heavy weight, it may get wet and it must not collapse if it does, it must look attractive and the cheaper it is the better. So, even with this simple problem, we are able to pursue a variety of channels – the scientific, the aesthetic and the economic. It really is important that the material used is strong enough for the job, even when it is wet. A fully technological approach would require the setting up of scientific investigations to produce the information we need. However, the scientific investigation is only being used to support the technological problem solving activity. That is how scientific activity is related to technological activity: it provides vital information which is fed into the problem solving process, along with the information which comes from looking at the problem with the eye of the artist or that of the economist.

Sophisticated technological problem solving is very demanding: children can only be introduced to the ideas and be helped to acquire in some measure the skills needed to set about a task. As soon as the task is within the children's grasp, they should use their increasing scientific skills to produce information needed to make decisions within the problem solving sequence. It should be clear that the kind of scientific information required will depend on the problem and the materials which might be used. A question about what kind of paper to use or whether plastic sheet would be better than paper can be answered from the scientific viewpoint by setting up an appropriate investigation. For some problems, the children might need information about whether to use wood or metal, or what kind of wood or metal. Again, the information can come from a scientific investigation. How to make something move is another question which can be tackled, or how to cut a sleeve so that the arm can move freely requires an investigation of how our limbs work. All these are examples of scientific investigation being used within the context of technological problem solving.

Technological problem solving or Making and doing can best be tackled systematically and in each of the activities suggested, the same structured but simple approach has been used. It is not intended, however, that this should be regarded as prescriptive; rather, it is indicative.

1 The problem
The statement of the problem to be solved.
2 Exploring the problem
Examining the nature of the problem and identifying the various face
of it; being quite sure that the nature of the problem is understood;
ensuring that the problem statement expresses the need.
3 Ideas for solving the problem
a) Producing ideas without, at this stage, being concerned with
whether they are practical; thinking creatively and openly; letting
original thinking loose; brainstorming.
b) Sifting the ideas; looking for obvious snags; comparing the ideas
c) Deciding which idea to pursue.
4 Making
Planning how to implement the chosen solution; collecting and, if
necessary, investigating methods of construction and materials. (Of
course, it is possible that unforeseen snags will be found which will
require that the solution chosen should be reconsidered. This
illustrates another aspect of technological problem solving – it is not
straightforward sequence. As the problem and its solution are pursue
there will be snags, new bits of information and new ideas which wi
require that steps be retraced and new and different decisions made.
Finally, craft skills are exercised in the making of the solution. The
skills of young children will be limited and imperfect but the aim is th
they should produce their solution to the best of their ability. Often,
idea will be far better than its execution. Our main interest is in the
development of technological thinking. At this stage, lack of
craftsmanship is, therefore, a secondary consideration although
teachers will undoubtedly wish to give children every help and
encouragement to improve their craft skills. Equally, teachers will be
concerned to ensure that every child experiences success, however
modest.
5 Evaluating
Does the chosen solution solve the problem? In the light of experien
would a different solution have been implemented? Might any of the
ideas which were rejected have been better? Do the children want to
try again? How have other people tackled similar problems?
At first, children will not find it easy to evaluate their own work.
Looking critically comes with maturity and for young children the
sense of the product being right because it is a personal achievemen
understandably overwhelming. Later, the children are able to look at
their own work and the work of others more circumspectly, and then
the teacher can (by question and discussion) help children to look a
their own work and the work of others in a more analytical fashion.
They are able to learn from each other and support each other's
thinking. It is a field rich in opportunities.

Monitoring making and doing activity

It has not been suggested that teachers should attempt to record forma
the development of children's making and doing skills; however, it ma
be useful to have in mind some questions which will help in monitoring
the children's progress. More importantly, the questions may be of
assistance in guiding the children's work. The questions are to some
extent ordered so that they indicate a developing competency, but they
should be regarded as no more than indicative. Tackling making and
doing problems has so many facets that it is not possible to identify a
right way or even a best way.
It is difficult also to suggest how children will progress. Some will
move slowly, some rapidly. Young children can be surprisingly innovat
and imaginative, particularly when they are interacting with constructi
materials. However, the level of thinking suggested by some of the
questions is sophisticated and may be reached by only a few children.
Nevertheless, the questions will provide a useful guide to progress in
making and doing activity.

1 The problem
2 Exploring the problem
   Do the children make little or no attempt to explore the problem?
   Do they ask one or two isolated questions?
   Do their questions go beyond what is immediately apparent?
   Do the children begin to ask questions more systematically and to identify criteria which must be met?
   Do the children, as a matter of course, ask a wide range of pertinent questions and assemble the criteria thus identified in an ordered manner?
   Can the children reframe the statement of the problem if the criteria identified indicate that this is necessary?
3 Ideas for solving the problem – choosing a solution to implement
   Do the children provide no ideas of their own and wait for ideas to be provided?
   Do they produce no ideas of their own but respond to and develop ideas that are provided?
   Do they produce one or two ideas of their own?
   Do they think freely and creatively if they are encouraged to do so?
   Do they attempt to evaluate ideas according to their understanding of the problem?
   Are they able to evaluate the ideas in relation to the material and skill resources which are available?
4 Making
   (The development of the ability to produce the chosen solution will depend on the nature of the artefacts being produced. Craft skills appropriate to the materials being used will be developed. Their development will relate closely to the development of attitudes to the work, as well as to the understanding and knowledge associated with the materials and solution chosen.)
   Do the children choose appropriate materials?
   Do they work neatly and safely with these materials?
   Do the children use appropriate tools in the correct manner, thinking of their own safety and that of others?
   Do they work accurately?
   Do they use materials imaginatively?
   Are they able to improvise?
5 Evaluating
   Do the children make no attempt to evaluate their own work?
   Do they attempt to evaluate their own work in some measure?
   Do they view their own work with some detachment and examine it with some degree of analysis?
   Do they consider criticisms of their own work by others?
   Do the children look at their products critically and consider whether they meet the criteria identified in exploring the problem?
   Are they able to suggest how the product might be improved?

Extension G People and their jobs and occupations

On page 98, you will find this statement:
'Science is used in society in all sorts of ways. People use it in their work and hobbies. Everyone is confronted with it in everyday life.'
A variety of people who do different work and have different hobbies are introduced in the scheme, in order to show how science is important for them all. The kinds of work and hobbies they have were chosen with the following criteria in mind:
1 relevance to children of this age range and breadth of experience;
2 the relative importance of science in the particular work or hobby;
3 potential as a context for the development of science activities and understanding of ideas.
'Work' refers not only to paid work but also to all that work which is given little recognition because it is not financially rewarded. Therefore, the word 'job' has been used to signify paid work and 'occupation' to signify unpaid work. What are jobs for some are occupations or hobbies for others, and this might have to be pointed out. Here are parts of the original lists:

Jobs
School caretaker, school cook, lollipop man or lady, policeman or woman, detective, forensic scientist, firefighter, optician, hairdresser, health visitor, school doctor, general practitioner, nurse, dentist, medical auxiliary, engineer (aeronautical, electrical, electronic, etc.), chemist (plastics, fibres, food, etc.), pharmacist, public analyst, gardener, electrician, joiner, painter, decorator, motor mechanic, shop assistant, jeweller.

Occupations
Housewife, mother, father, DIY activities . . .

Hobbies
Fishing, flower arranging, pottery, athletics, pop music, playing the guitar (piano, violin, etc.), swimming, games . . .

It was after drawing up the lists that it became apparent that a good opportunity would be missed if there was no discussion about what jobs, occupations and hobbies are and what people do when they are pursuing their various interests. What is it that makes people want to do these things? What is it that makes them worthwhile?

Below are points which the children should be made aware of; these points have been used in drawing up the suggestions for discussions. The points listed are very basic ones because very many children have little idea about jobs and occupations. Often, even parents do not talk to their children about the work they do in their jobs and occupations.
1 People work.
2 Sometimes work is done in return for money (jobs). Sometimes work is unpaid (occupations).
3 Different people do different jobs and follow different occupations.
4 The work of some people helps us directly.
5 The work of some people helps us indirectly – they work behind the scenes.
6 Some work is done just during the day. Some work has to be done at special times.
7 Some work has to be done all the time.
8 Some jobs are not very pleasant but they serve the community.
9 People take pride in their work.
10 People may need special knowledge, expertise and skills in their work and hobbies.
11 People have to acquire the special knowledge, expertise and skills which they need.
12 People only work in jobs for part of the time.

13 When people are not working at jobs, they do other things and follow other occupations and hobbies which they enjoy.

14 Sometimes, people's enjoyment depends on the jobs being done by other people.

15 What is a job for one person may be an occupation or hobby for another.

16 People use scientific information in their jobs, occupations and hobbies.

17 People need to use a scientific viewpoint in their jobs, occupations and hobbies.

Extension H   Recording progress in science

There are two aspects of children's progress which should be recorded:
1 their experience of scientific ideas – ideas which they have encountered in the activities;
2 their progress in acquiring the skills being developed in the activities.

Ongoing accurate records are an essential part of ensuring that children' experience of science is progressive and developmental; to assist teachers in keeping records, sets of pupils' *Record Sheets* are available. There is a *Record Sheet* for each level so that a complete record of progress can be maintained for each pupil and accompany him or her from one class to the next.

Experience of scientific ideas

The science concepts and ideas covered in the topic activities are shown in Table 3 in Extension B of *Science through Infant Topics, Teachers' Books A, B and C*. The experiences provided by each of the activities are described briefly in Extension C (*Teachers' Books A, B* and *C*).

Science skills

The science skills developed in the scheme are shown in Table 2 in Extension A (*Teachers' Books A, B* and *C*).

On the back of each *Record Sheet*, the skill levels which the children should ideally have reached by the end of Levels 1 and 2 are described. On the front of the *Record Sheets* the skills are listed accompanied by a series of boxes. The boxes cover a range of comments, from 'not yet able' for children who are a long way off reaching the described skill level to 'competently' for those children who can perform in the manner described. In between, the boxes allow you to make qualified responses (ticking as appropriate), matching the child's ability to the skill description.

There is a bar in the line of boxes at a point which might represent a resonable level of competence to be achieved by all children.

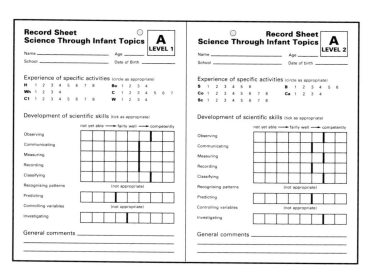

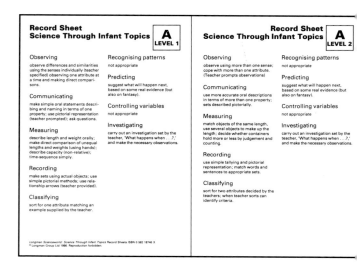

Extension I Classroom organisation

Preparation

Before each half term, you might find it a good idea to decide which topics and which specific activities you intend to cover, go through the equipment required (Extension J, page 137) and also read the 'You need' section for each of your activities. Then you can collect together the items you need and look for any you do not have immediately to hand.

You may find it useful also to make up boxes for the activities so that you have everything in one place. Boxes can contain unique items, common items and a note of any other items which need to be collected from elsewhere to complete the set of equipment.

Another method of organisation is to keep a card index, with a card for each activity. This could list the items required for the activity and say where they are to be found. Coloured cards for special items which may need to be located well in advance could be put in 'early warning' positions, so that you have enough time to prepare.

Before embarking on an activity with the children, you will need to read the notes in the *Teachers' Book* carefully so that you are familiar with the objectives and the approach. As you become increasingly accustomed to using the scheme, you may be tempted to skim through the notes: this is not advisable as you may miss important details referring to secondary objectives. Often, the odd question or comment is particularly significant. Also, the detail is intended to guide you in making the gradual change of approach which the children's developing skills and confidence require.

Organising the work

Although some of the activities will lend themselves to a class lesson or discussion, most of the activities are intended for groups of four to eight children. This way of working is familiar to most infant teachers, as are the two practical problems which arise: how to organise the rest of the class so that you can spend some relatively uninterrupted time with one group; and how to prevent the children in the rest of the class observing what is going on so that when their turn comes they already know what it is all about. They may see the result before the problem. Many teachers will have found their own solutions; if you are still searching for an answer, you might like to consider the following suggestions.

1 **How can you organise the class so that you are free to work with a small group?**

   a) Use other people

   You may have time when a helper employed in the school works with you in the classroom. This may be a trained person, e.g. approved by the National Nursery Examination Board, or an ancillary helper. You can concentrate on your science group while your helper monitors the work of the rest of the children and deals with any minor difficulties.

   If you work in an open plan or semi-open plan building you may be able to organise team teaching, so that groups are shared unevenly between staff at certain times, allowing a small science group to be formed.

   Finally, you may be able to organise volunteer help which will free you to concentrate on your science group.

   b) If you have no help

   You can arrange your class so that children are working on some less teacher intensive activities while you are working with your science group. Make a list of activities which the children can do without a lot of help. These may include some of the following, depending on the children's ages and abilities:

   Free play with apparatus and/or materials prior to or following their more structured use, e.g. sand, water, paint, construction toys, etc.

   Reading for enjoyment at a level that the children can cope with easily.

Matching and fitting activities which are self-correcting.

Practising skills for improved neatness or learning useful facts, e.g. handwriting, number bonds, etc.

Making observational drawings of materials which are used for an activity.

Some craft activities can be pursued once the basic skills have been acquired, e.g. weaving, knitting, etc.

2 **How can you arrange your class so that the children do not know the outcome of the science activities before they do them?**

Arrange your classroom furniture to form a bay or bays. This allows a variety of work to go on without one thing interfering with another. I can also make the room look more interesting, with opportunities for good display related to specific aspects of the children's work.

When a new activity is introduced, choose a different group each time to be the first to do it.

Use corridors, wide entrances or any other nearby spaces which can supervised properly and where you do not get in anyone's way, but where the science group can work without acting like a magnet for everyone else.

It may be possible for groups of older children to tackle different activities and then come together as a class to explain to the rest of the class what they did and what they found out.

Keeping records and evaluating work

The pupils' *Record Sheets* for the scheme are described on page 134. These are quite easy to keep and require just a little time to be spent at the end of each level. However, as you carry out the work with the children you will find it helpful to note down briefly their reactions and response to the work. You can prepare a rough table which includes the names of the children in the group, the various objectives of the activity, and headings such as 'involvement' or 'enthusiasm'. You can quickly tick, cross or comment in your own shorthand as the activity progresses. You rough table might look like this:

Names	Sorting by size	Sorting by colour	Involvement	Comments
John	✗	✓ could match to mine	✓	No idea of longer/shorter
Steven	✓	✓	?	too easy
Jane	✓	✓ knew names	✓	found it easy
Amanda	✗	✓ matched	✓	Needs longer/shorter

This will be helpful in filling in the *Record Sheets* and in planning the next work. In this case, John and Amanda are going to need more 'longer/shorter' experiences; Steven and Jane may be able to join another group and miss some of the activities concerned with colour and size.

It should now be easier with this developmental scheme to match a child's work to his or her particular needs.

Extension J   Equipment and techniques

Part 1 Equipment, materials and storage
  a) Equipment and materials
  b) Storage
Part 2 Techniques
  a) Growing plants and seeds
  b) Keeping animals
  c) Simple electrical circuits

Part 1   Equipment, materials and storage

a) Equipment and materials

The science activities described do not require very much specialised equipment or apparatus. All the activities can be carried out in the classroom, in its vicinity or in the playground. For a number of activities, access to water and a power point are required, while for a few others you need a refrigerator or an oven for a short time. Much of what you need will already be in school and most of the rest can be borrowed from home, although you will no doubt find it more convenient to establish a store of the more commonly used items in school. The problem of storage is discussed in the next section.

  The materials and equipment which you will need for the infant years are listed on the following pages. Any additional requirements for a particular activity are listed in the description of the activity.

Classroom equipment and materials
The following equipment and supplies which are normally required in infant teaching should be included:

Apparatus and equipment
construction sets (including Lego and Meccano)
water play apparatus (including watering cans, sieves, funnels, transparent plastic tubing and waterproof aprons)
sand play apparatus with fine dry sand
playhouse facilities
musical instruments (particularly percussion, including sleigh bells)

Consumable materials
a variety of paper (including kitchen, blotting, tissue, crêpe and sugar papers)
drawing and colouring materials (including chalk, wax crayons, drawing charcoal and an ink pad)
modelling materials (including plasticine and clay)
adhesives (including polyvinyl adhesive)
paper clips (wire and brass)
string, twine of various kinds
rubber bands
adhesive labels
Blutak
sellotape
wallpaper paste
drinking straws and art straws

General household equipment and materials
cling film
aluminium foil
polythene bags (small and large rolls)
greaseproof paper
brown wrapping paper
paper towels (kitchen roll)

tissues
thin plastic sheet (dry cleaning covers, shop bags, etc.)
black dustbin liners
parcel tape
cocktail sticks
needles and pins
cotton and threads
safety pins
stapler

Kitchen equipment and supplies

a large electric hot plate (big enough to accommodate two glass pans; you could substitute other means of heating which would not be as safe or as satisfactory; you could regard this as the one big investment you need to make.)
two or three glass pans (coffee making flasks could also be used. Glass laboratory beakers can be substituted but they are more fragile.)
a variety of bowls, jugs, plates, dishes, etc. (of various shapes, sizes, materials, e.g. plastic, pottery, stainless steel, aluminium, heatproof glass some identical pairs and some sets would be useful. Most of these can brought from home as required. However, you may feel it necessary to make some purchases to provide variety and matching pairs, and to cater for the needs of two groups who want things at the same time.)
a variety of cups and beakers (various shapes, sizes, materials, e.g. transparent and opaque plastic, pottery, paper, heatproof glass, etc.)
a variety of cutlery (metal and plastic, of different sizes)
a collection of cooking implements (wooden spoons, tin openers, bottle openers, perforated spoons, sieves, colanders, rolling pins, pastry cutter funnels, etc.)
a collection of cooking equipment (baking tray, patty/tart/bun tins, mixing bowl, pastry boards, kitchen scales)
a tablecloth
trays (metal and non-metal)
ice cube tray

Foodstuffs

flour
rice
sugar (granulated, caster, icing, crystal)
salt
cooking oil
food colouring

Garden equipment and supplies

potting compost (peat based for convenience)

Workshop equipment and supplies

hammers (three sizes)
screwdrivers (three or four different lengths)
nails (a range of at least three head sizes and lengths; different metals – iron, brass, zinc; same sizes in different metals where possible.)
screws (a range of at least three head sizes and lengths; different metal steel, brass, aluminium; same sizes in different metals where possible.)
small saws

Junk

A major requirement for a class of children who are enthusiastically pursuing scientific and technological activities is a large, varied, motivating and never-ending supply of junk. A stock of junk should include:
newspapers and magazines
plastic sheet and bags (all sizes, all thicknesses)
paper of all kinds (wallpaper particularly)
corrugated cardboard
jars and bottles with and without screw caps (all shapes and sizes, glass

and plastic, rigid and squeezy)
soap or hand cream dispensers
egg boxes
cheese boxes
cuboid boxes (large and small; with and without lids; plastic, wood,
cardboard, metal)
sweet jars (plastic, preferably)
plastic food trays
plastic cartons (yoghurt, margarine, etc.)
aluminium foil dishes, trays and cartons
pieces of fabric (any shape or size; any fibre type, colour or texture)
pieces of floor coverings (cork, vinyl, tiles of all kinds, carpet)
cardboard tube (toilet rolls, kitchen rolls)
expanded polystyrene (pieces of block, tile, packaging, etc.)
bottle tops
plastic beer glasses (transparent – one pint)
plastic cups and beakers (transparent, opaque, expanded polystyrene,
double sided)
pieces of wood (particularly soft wood of small cross-section)
metal
plastic

Collecting junk
Every teacher can use parents, friends, the school kitchen and local shops
as a rich supply of containers, boxes and the like. Particularly useful to
remember are:
wine shops – the strongest cardboard containers with useful
compartments, some packing materials;
furniture shops – large cardboard containers, large sheets of strong
plastic, bubble plastic packing sheets;
white goods suppliers – large cardboard cartons, polystyrene packaging;
DIY shops – bits and off-cuts of all sorts of materials;
paint and wallpaper shops – out-of-date pattern books, colour cards,
damaged polystyrene tiles, odd rolls of wallpaper, etc;
timber merchants – off-cuts of all kinds of wood cross-sections, lengths
of soft wood which children can saw (dowel rod, lathe), different kinds
of wood;
monumental mason – bits both rough and polished of a variety of stone,
marble and granite.

Less often considered or exploited as a source of junk are local
companies, particularly manufacturing companies. They produce all sorts
of material which is waste for them but of value to schools. Companies
do not want waste material left lying around so it is quickly destroyed if it
does not find a better home.

Why not see if you can come to an arrangement with local companies,
and put some of their junk to good use? You probably pass companies on
your way to school and there may be some in the area surrounding the
school. You could write to them or, better still, call in. Most people will be
glad to help in some way and you will have found a reason to make
contact and establish a link between your school and the company. That
can bear fruit in all sorts of ways: inviting the people from the company to
visit your school; you and maybe the children visiting the company; more
information about people and their jobs; more examples of people using
science; and more ideas for topic work.

Science equipment
magnifying glasses (a large, flexible arm, table mounted, magnifying
glass is useful. Hand lenses should be readily available, and there is a
range of magnifiers for observing specimens – some form the lids of small
specimen boxes.)
binocular microscope (invaluable item)
large mirror (to put flat on the table)
small hand mirrors
large and small standard magnets
one or two pairs of strong magnets (Alnico or similar)

torch bulbs
torch batteries
plastic covered bell wire } to make electric circuit
bulb holders
crocodile clips
tape recorder
camera
two thermometers
  (marked in degrees Celsius)

Mathematics apparatus
sorting circles
2D and 3D plastic/wooden shapes (large and small)
2D templates for regular shapes
30 cm rulers (unmarked and marked 10 cm, 20 cm and 30 cm)
metre sticks (unmarked and marked)
one litre and half litre measuring jars
balance scales
bucket balance
callipers

Certain other apparatus is used during the scheme:

Year 1	Year 2	Year 3
poleido blocks	posting box	set of weights 10 g–1 kg
coloured beads and laces	matrix diagram	several gram weights
sorting trays	sorting tree	1 g–10 g
large arrows	egg timer	tape measures
	clock	minute timer
	card arrows	

b) Storage

Central storage or classroom storage
Various problems arise in planning how to store science equipment and
materials. Firstly, a decision has to be taken as to whether to establish a
central store or whether to store equipment and materials in each
classroom. This will depend on the particular circumstances of your own
school but certain requirements and considerations will be common.
Infrequently used specialised equipment is certainly better kept in a
central store to which all teachers have access. For more generally used
small scale equipment and materials it makes sense to arrange storage in
individual classrooms; however, it is most important that someone should
make a record of what is where, and that everyone concerned has access
to this record. The person who keeps the record should also be
responsible for ensuring that equipment is maintained in a serviceable
condition and that materials are replaced.

Activity boxes
It may be advantageous to collect together the equipment needed for a
particular activity and to put it in its own labelled box so that it is available
for anyone wishing to use that activity. The box can contain specific
items and a note of anything else that is needed to complete the set of
equipment for that activity.

   Various boxes, trays and cartons made from card or plastic can be
purchased commercially but there is a wide range of useful containers
available free from a variety of sources. Shoe shops can provide a variety
of smaller boxes while greengrocers have stacking boxes, e.g. tomato
boxes, which can be most useful.

Pupil access to materials
The biggest headache is trying to make satisfactory arrangements for the
storage of equipment, material and junk to which pupils should have
access. It requires considerable thought to devise a system which gives
encouraging and necessary freedom of access but at the same time
affords reasonable security for equipment.

Junk in particular takes up a lot of room and needs to be neatly stored if it is not to overflow in all directions. Again, commercially produced storage boxes, bins and containers can be attractive but strong cardboard boxes, e.g. wine shop boxes, can be stacked between solid walls or pieces of furniture to form a storage range. They can be placed in the classroom or in a wide corridor – but do check that you are not contravening fire or safety regulations.

…torage range

Small items can be stored in plastic containers which have had a corner cut away. They are free, look tidy and are easy to store side by side on a shelf.

cut

…stic container used for storage

The important thing is that the materials are to hand and that children are not held up for want of a jam jar of the right size or a yoghurt carton. Children, like teachers, will appreciate a system which is maintained in an orderly fashion so that everyone knows where things should be and finds that they are there. That in itself is good education.

Part 2 Techniques

a) Growing plants and seeds

A number of activities involve growing plants and seeds. These are particularly rewarding activities not only because of the scientific/observational interest but also because they give children the opportunity to take individual responsibility for the care of a living thing. Below are some very basic guidelines which will help to ensure success. If you want more detailed information you should consult a gardening book or a local garden centre.

Compost
Seeds and plants need something to grow in. In the garden, they grow in soil but in the confinement of a pot or box they are likely to flourish better if planted in a specially prepared compost. There are basically two different types of compost: peat-based or loamless (various brands, e.g. Levington's), and loam-based (John Innes composts, which are sold made up under many trade names).

Each type of compost has different grades, depending on whether it is intended for seed-sowing, small plants in small pots or large plants in large pots. There are also general purpose composts. For classroom use, you will find a peat-based general purpose compost most suitable and convenient. The peat-based composts are clean to use and light in weight for their bulk. It should be noted, however, that if plants are to be grown on for more than two or three months, feeding is necessary. Peat itself does not contain plant nutrients and the compost relies on added substances, which need to be replaced as the plant grows.

Growing plants

Pots or boxes for plant growing must have good drainage: yoghurt cartons etc. should have holes punched in their bases, and the pots should not be left to stand in puddles of water. Plastic food trays are useful for standing pots on. Virtually anything can be used as a container provided it has good drainage. Most plants object strongly to having their roots water-logged and more plants probably die of over-watering than under-watering. Generally, if you have any doubt about when to water, is better for the plant actually to look as if it needs water than to give it too much. Some plants, however, do object to being allowed to go dry and plants which are flowering or growing freely usually require much more water than slow growing or dormant plants. Also, plants can cope with more water when they are in a warm place than when they are in a cold one.

Plants which like dry conditions, e.g. cacti and succulents (fleshy leaved plants), are best kept in clay pots (with a specially prepared compost) but most other plants are quite happy in plastic pots and general purpose compost.

Plants should be planted firmly with thumb pressure on the compost, but the compost should not be packed down. They should be fed with a liquid fertilizer (or other pot plant fertilizer) about once a fortnight.

Small plants need small pots and most flowering plants flower best if kept in pots which appear to be full of roots. Eventually, a plant will need repotting when it gets too big for its pot. Likely signs are that it stops growing, its pot seems very full of roots and it looks unhappy. Plants should only be repotted during the growing season and a plant should be transferred to a pot which is only slightly bigger than the old one. Before repotting, the plant should be on the dry side and the new compost should not be too wet since after repotting the plant should be carefully watered. Repotting is a shock process for plants and they need sympathetic treatment.

Repotting

root mass

root mass

new compost

Some plants like bright light and some prefer shade. Very few like strong direct sunlight and most hate draughts. Finding out where plants are happy is often a trial and error matter. Reference books will tell you whether a species of plant is a sun or shade lover and what temperature requires, but after that it really is a case of trying the plant in different places until you find a spot where it is happy (i.e. grows, keeps its leaves and maintains a good leaf colour). If any plant is not thriving try moving to various places in the room since even very small differences in the amount of light can affect the plant's well-being considerably.

Growing seeds

Seeds need warmth and moisture for germination. After germination, they also need light and ventilation. Seeds such as peas and beans which can be handled individually should be planted about 4 cm deep, in well moistened compost. Finer seeds should be nearer the surface, and very small seeds should be sprinkled on the surface of the moist compost and covered with a very thin layer of fine compost.

The seed pots or boxes should be covered with cling film and put in a warm place (but not in direct sun) with newspaper over the top. As soon as the seeds germinate, the newspaper and the cling film should be removed but a loose covering of plastic sheet may be useful in conserving moisture. Tiny seedlings need to be watered (sprayed) very gently. They need plenty of light but avoid direct sunlight in the early stages. For growing on instructions, you should consult the seed packet.

Sprouting bean shoots

Various kinds of seeds which can be used to produce bean sprouts can be obtained from health food stores. The following method produces good results.

The ideal container is a square fruit juice bottle but any similar wide-necked jar can be used. The mouth of the jar should be covered with a piece of muslin, surgical gauze or similar, held in place with a rubber band. To start the beans off, the jar is rinsed with water and most of the water drained out. About 1 level dessertspoonful of seed is put in the jar and tossed about, so that the wet seeds stick to the sides of the jar. With the muslin cover in place, the jar is put in a warm, dark cupboard.

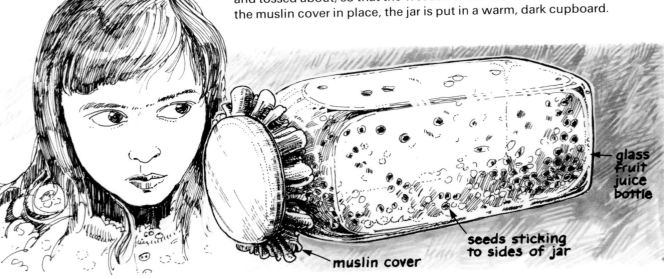

glass fruit juice bottle

seeds sticking to sides of jar

muslin cover

The seeds or shoots should be washed with clean water and drained twice a day until the bean shoots are the desired length – about 4 to 6 cm. This will take only a few days, the exact time depending on the variety. You will find more information on the seed packet.

b) Keeping animals

Keeping animals in the classroom is very worthwhile not only as a focus for science activity but also as a source of pleasure and satisfaction for the children. Children can gain a great deal from having an animal to care for at school. The children should be responsible for the care of the animals, and great emphasis should be placed on the idea that these small creatures rely entirely on the children for their well-being.

There are a number of activities which allow the study of animals and fish but observation of the creatures and their behaviour should continue throughout the year. The animal cages and fish tanks should not become just part of the classroom furniture.

For details of housing, feeding and care of animals and fish you should consult one of the many specialised books or pamphlets which are available (see reference list). The following notes may help you in deciding which animals to keep.

Rabbits

They are particularly good for younger children – easy to handle, not eas[y] to lose in a classroom as they are not too quick, they sit still long enough for the children to have a really good look at any particular feature, and they do not bite. However, they need a big hutch and as they are not completely indoor animals they need access to outdoor pens. They smel[l] very little. Arranging for their care at weekends and holidays can be a problem. Rabbit hutches are not easily transportable.

Guinea pigs

As for rabbits, but they can live indoors all the time. They are ideal for younger children. They do not smell, they do not bite and the cage is small enough to transport easily to its 'holiday home'. If the cage is put [on] a sand tray the guinea pigs can be left to potter in and out and they develop very clean habits. They are nervous animals though, and can suffer from over handling.

Both rabbits and guinea pigs make small puddles if free in the classroom but no more than a floor-cloth is needed.

Hamsters and gerbils

Hamsters and gerbils are small and attractive. There is no smell, and little in the way of puddles although they can have accidents. They move ver[y] quickly and are easy to lose behind cupboards etc. They can bite; hamsters are nocturnal animals and can become aggressive if continuall[y] disturbed during the daytime. With gerbils, the pregnant females, nursin[g] mothers and very small young can be handled without any ill effects.

Rats

They are intelligent and make good pets. They appreciate spacious wooden housing where they can move easily (they can grow as large as [a] small rabbit), and explore their surroundings.

Mice

Mice are very appealing but they move very quickly and are easy for sma[ll] children to lose. Unfortunately, they do smell.

Note:

1 Classroom animals can carry bacteria harmful to human beings and children must be taught to wash their hands after handling the animal[s] and particularly before eating.

2 Monkeys, squirrels and other wild animals should not be kept as classroom pets because they constitute a health hazard.
3 Budgerigars can on rare occasions be carriers of psittacosis and for this reason it is best not to keep them in a classroom which is occupied all the time by the children. A secure, draught free position in a corridor or school hall where children can enjoy observing them without prolonged contact in a confined space may be a possibility.

Budgerigars should be purchased from a breeder with an established stock; problems seem to arise where birds are imported from the wild.

Some Local Education Authorities make specific recommendations about where the birds should be housed and others have banned them from schools, so you should check your own position. It is recommended that the birds are kept in pairs and housed in an aviary large enough for them to spread their wings and to provide an area of privacy.

For the science activities suggested in the scheme, you might like to borrow a budgerigar from a parent or friend if you do not already have one in school.

c) Simple electrical circuits

Below are some basic notes about simple electrical circuits of the kind used in torches.

In a torch, a battery and a bulb are joined by conducting material to form a circuit. A switch is incorporated so that the circuit can be closed and the bulb will light.

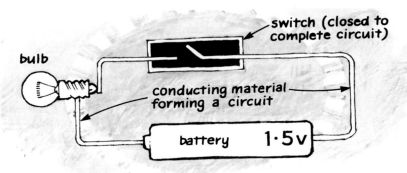

The battery

The battery is the electricity store. When a circuit is formed, the battery pushes the electricity through the circuit. How hard it pushes is measured in volts. The batteries which are used in torches are usually 1.5 volt batteries. If two are arranged inside the torch in line, the push is 3 volts. Batteries can be arranged in other ways so that the voltages are added. This battery is a 3 volt battery.

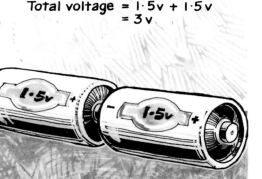

Total voltage = 1.5v + 1.5v
= 3v

Total voltage = 1.5v + 1.5v
= 3v

Batteries up to about 12 volts are quite safe for classroom use but for simple work you will not need more than a 3 volt battery.

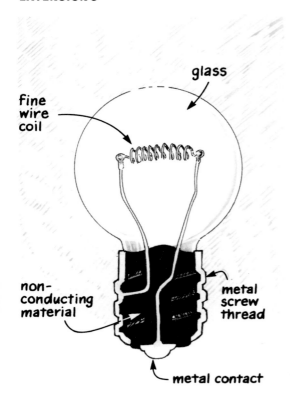

The bulb

A bulb looks like the drawing on the left.

The space inside the bulb contains no air and there is a very fine wire which is coiled and the ends fastened to the side and end of the bulb. (I is easier to see the coil in a normal clear light bulb.) When electricity passes through the bulb filament, it becomes extremely hot and glows white hot – and so gives out light. How brightly it glows depends partly on how hard the electricity is being pushed through, i.e. it depends on th voltage of the battery. Torch bulbs are rated according to the battery which will make them light up well, so they are labelled with a voltage; the voltage of the bulb should match the voltage of the battery within narrow limits. If the voltage of the battery is much above the voltage of the bulb, the filament in the bulb will become overheated and break. Always check that bulb and battery match (or nearly).

> e.g. 1.25 volt bulb with 1.5 volt battery (maximum)
>   2.5 volt bulb with 3 volt battery (maximum)

The conducting material

The conducting material is always metal – wire, strip or even part of the torch case. The metal contact at the end of the bulb usually touches one terminal of the battery directly.

Note:
1 A material which is not a conductor is a non-conductor.
2 Arbitrarily, a very effective non-conductor is called an insulator.

The switch

In a torch, this is merely a mechanical means of making or breaking the circuit. If there is a physical gap in the circuit, the bulb can only be switched on if the gap is bridged by a conducting material.

The circuit

When the switch is closed there is a continuous path of conducting material from one terminal of the battery through the bulb and back to th other terminal of the battery. Only when the circuit is complete can a current flow and the bulb light up.

Setting up a circuit in the classroom

A 3 volt battery is suitable for making connections. The connections to i can be secured either by crocodile clips or paper clips. N.B. The covering at the ends of the wires must be removed so that connections are to bare wire.

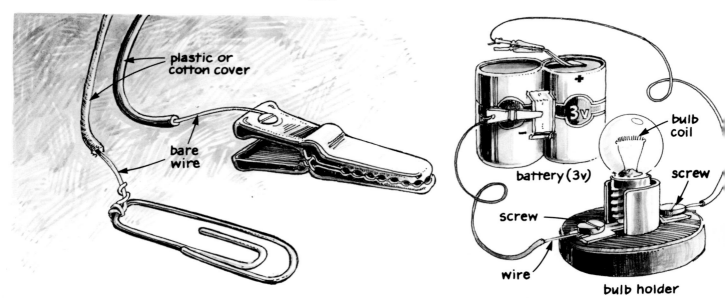

It is easier to make good connections to the bulb if the bulb is put into bulb holder. The bulb holder takes the wire from one screw to one end o the bulb coil and the wire from the other screw goes to the other end of the bulb coil.

An elaborate switch is not necessary. Paper clips and drawing pins can be used for perfectly satisfactory switches.

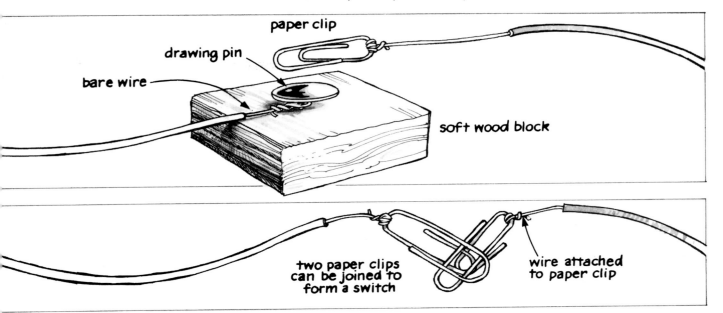

paper clip

drawing pin

bare wire

soft wood block

two paper clips
can be joined to
form a switch

wire attached
to paper clip

Some useful reference material

Teachers' books

School science policy

The DES Assessment of Performance Unit (APU) has published various reports and documents on science education. These include:

Science in Schools. Age 11: Report No. 3, DES 1984
Science Assessment Framework. Age 11: Report No. 4, HMSO 1984

Copies of these reports and others in the series are available from: The Association for Science Education, College Lane, Hatfield, Hertfordshire, AL10 9AA.

DES, *Science 5–16: A Statement of Policy*, HMSO 1985
Formulating a School Policy: with an Index to Science 5–13, (*Learning through Science Project*), Macdonald Educational 1980

Resources

Bainbridge J W, Stockdale R W and Wastnedge E R, *Junior Science Source Book*, Collins 1970
Science Resources for Primary and Middle Schools, (*Learning through Science Project*), Macdonald Educational 1982

Living things

Animals in Schools, 2nd edn, RSPCA 1985
Gregory V B A, *Keeping of Animals and Plants in School*, RSPCA 1985.
A variety of books, leaflets and posters on the care of animals and plants are available from the RSPCA and from the Schools Natural Science Society.
RSPCA publications from local pet shops or from Royal Society for the Prevention of Cruelty to Animals Education Department, Causeway, Horsham, West Sussex RH12 1HG.
Schools Natural Science Society publications from The Association for Science Education.

Animals and plants, Nuffield Junior Science Project, Collins 1967

People and their jobs and occupations

A source of excellent, well-presented information is the COIC (Careers and Occupational Information Centre), Moorfoot, Sheffield S1 4PQ. The *Working in . . .* series in particular provides bright, colourful material giving information for the teacher and attractive pictures for display. Local Education Authority careers service offices will be able to provide examples of this material.

More ideas for science activities and help with science teaching

Finch I, *Nature study and science*, Longman 1971
Kincaid D and Coles P S, *Science in a Topic* series, Hulton Educational 1973
Science 5–13 series, Macdonald Educational 1972
Teaching Primary Science series, Macdonald Educational 1975

Children's books

A variety of topics

Gulliford R, *Stop, look, listen, Teachers' booklet*
This booklet accompanies the television programme *Stop, look, listen* and provides useful book lists for each topic covered in the series. The booklet can be ordered through Central Television, Central House, Broad Street, Birmingham B1 2JP.
Ivory L A, *Headstart* series, Burke 1970
Let's Go series, Franklyn Watts 1974
My First Library series, Macdonald Educational 1984
Pluckrose H (ed), *Small World* series, Hamish Hamilton 1979
Whitlock R and Heeks P, *Down on the Farm* series, Wayland 1984

Living things

Althea, *Life Cycle* series, Longman 1977
Althea, *Animals at Home* series, Dinosaur Publications 1981
Moon C, *In the Wild* series, Wayland 1983
Observing Nature series, Wayland 1980

People and their jobs and occupations

Stewart A, *Cherrystone* series, Hamish Hamilton 1983
Swayne D and Savage P, *I am . . .* series, Dent 1978
Egan (ed), *When I Grow Up* (Benjamin Books series), adapted from the Dutch by Jan Selby, CIO Publications 1975

More ideas for science activities

Kincaid D and Coles P S, *Read and Do* series, Arnold Wheaton 1981
Science Starters series, Macdonald Educational 1983

Index

RECORD SHEETS: the record sheets on the inside front cover and inside back cover may be photocopied by the purchasers of this book.

Opposite, on the inside back cover, is the main record sheet, described below.

On the inside front cover is the reverse side of the record sheet, providing details of the skill levels.

On the pupils' *Record Sheets* two aspects of progress are recorded:

1 Experience of specific activities (scientific ideas)

This is recorded by circling the appropriate activity code.

H (1) 2 3 (4)(5) 6 7 8   Bo (1)(2) 3 4
Wh 1 (2)(3) 4   C 1 2 (3)(4) 5 6 (7)

2 Development of scientific skills

On the back of each *Record Sheet*, the skill levels which the children should ideally have reached by the end of Levels 1 and 2 are described. On the front of the *Record Sheets* the skills are listed accompanied by a series of boxes. The boxes cover a range of comments, from 'not yet able' for children who are a long way off reaching the described skill level to 'competently' for those children who can perform in the manner described. In between, the boxes allow you to make qualified responses (ticking as appropriate), matching the child's ability to the skill description.
    There is a bar in the line of boxes at a point which might represent a reasonable level of competence to be achieved by all children.

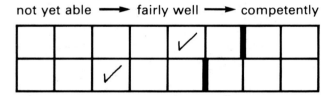

It would be advisable to pay particular attention to children or skills where there is evidence of performance below the level which we have indicated.
    It is intended that the *Record Sheets* should be completed at the end of a Level, but there is no reason why the blocks should not be filled in at more frequent intervals if you wish to do so.

Longman Scienceworld: Science Through Infant Topics Record Sheets

© Longman Group Ltd 1986.